THE LOVERS' PATH

Reading Tarot for Love and Relationships

By: Celeste Randall

Table of Contents

Introduction

"The best love is the kind that awakens the soul and makes us reach for more, that plants a fire in our hearts and brings peace to our minds." - Nicholas Sparks

Ah, *L'amore*! What could be sweeter?

Love is one of the most powerful emotions known to humans, and it has been a topic of fascination for centuries. From the works of William Shakespeare to the lyrics of modern-day pop songs, love has always been a popular subject. And there's a good reason for that! Love is not just important for our emotional well-being, but it is also a source of great fun and joy in our lives.

At its core, love is about forming connections with other people, whether it's romantic love or platonic love. These connections are what make life worth living. They give us a sense of purpose and belonging, and they help us navigate the ups and downs of life. In romantic relationships, love can be an incredible source of happiness, pleasure, and excitement. From the thrill of a first date to the comfort of a long-term partnership, love provides us with a sense of security and fulfillment that is hard to find anywhere else.

But love is not just about the good times. It also challenges us in ways that can help us grow and become better people. Love requires us to be vulnerable, to open ourselves up to the possibility of rejection or heartbreak. It forces us to confront our fears, insecurities, and flaws, and to work through them in order to build a stronger, healthier relationship. And when we do overcome these obstacles, the sense of accomplishment and satisfaction we feel is unparalleled.

But what do we do when we cannot overcome the obstacles we face in our relationships? To whom do we turn when our most beloved ones are mad at us, or us at them? Or when we have been betrayed? What recourse do we have when we are suspicious that a loved one is hiding something from us, or lying to us? What if, against all evidence to the contrary, our intuition about a person is nagging us that something is up behind the scenes? And what if we want to know where a new relationship is headed? Is the other person really interested in us, or are they just engaging in some meaningless flirting to pass the time?

If you were ever hoping there was a way to answer these questions and more, then I have great news for you! Using a combination of your own intuition and the symbology of the ancient Tarot, you can gain a deeper understanding of your love life and gain the upper hand in any situation your relationship may be facing.

With that said, I want to welcome you to the world of Tarot, where ancient symbolism meets modern divination! Tarot is a powerful tool that can offer insights and guidance in various aspects of life, including love and relationships. In this particular book, we will be exploring everything the Tarot has to offer with respect to love and relationships, specifically. Whether you are seeking answers about a current relationship, a potential romance, or trying to navigate through a difficult situation regarding a loved one, Tarot can provide valuable insights to help you make informed decisions and better understand the dynamics at play.

The history of Tarot dates back to the 15th century, where it was used as a playing card game in Italy. It wasn't until the 18th century that Tarot began to be used for divinatory purposes. Tarot was then popularized in the late 19th and early 20th centuries through the work of occultists and mystics, such as Aleister Crowley and Arthur Edward Waite. Today, Tarot has become a widely recognized and respected form of divination, used by people from all walks of life.

The use of Tarot as divinatory practice throughout history aimed to provide guidance through a multitude of life's problems and to answer pertinent questions. As you might imagine, many of those questions revolved around interpersonal relationships, as they play a crucial role in our lives. They provide us with love, companionship, and support.

We ask about our partners, our family members, our friends, our coworkers, and even our casual acquaintances. Healthy relationships can help us grow and evolve as individuals, while toxic relationships can have detrimental effects on our mental and emotional well-being. Given the significance of relationships, it's no surprise that people often turn to Tarot for guidance and insight.

People seek help from Tarot for many reasons, especially when it comes to love. Some may be looking for clarity and guidance about a current relationship or a potential romance, while others may be trying to make sense of a difficult situation, such as disagreements and anger between partners. Here are some other common reasons why people seek help from Tarot:

Love Triangles: Love triangles can be complicated and emotionally draining. People may seek guidance from Tarot to help them make sense of the situation and determine the best course of action.

Cheating: Infidelity can be devastating, and people may turn to Tarot to help them navigate through the complex emotions that arise from being cheated on or from being the one who has cheated.

Divorce: Divorce is a major life transition that can be emotionally and financially challenging. Tarot can offer guidance and clarity during this difficult time.

Flirting: Flirting can be exciting and fun, but it can also be confusing and misleading. Tarot can provide insights into the intentions of the other person and help individuals make informed decisions.

Marriage: Marriage is a significant commitment, and people may seek guidance from Tarot to help them navigate through the ups and downs of married life.

Romantic Interest: People may seek help from Tarot to gain insight into a potential romantic interest and whether the relationship has the potential to be successful.

Lack of communication: Many partners choose to cut off communication during difficult times in their relationships. Tarot can help us find out what the other person is thinking and feeling, even if they've gone radio silent.

As you can see, the potential to use Tarot to answer questions regarding love and relationships is extensive. There are a lot of aspects of our relationships that we can analyze using our little deck of 78 cards. This book, in particular, is designed to provide readers with a comprehensive understanding of how to use the Tarot for love and relationship readings, specifically.

This book will cover the basic meanings of each Tarot card, with a major emphasis on the meanings behind the cards as they pertain to love and relationships. These meanings are not always easily gleaned from the images, nor are they found in most Tarot books that provide classic interpretations; those general meanings tend to be confusing in the context of love and relationship questions (for instance, what, exactly, does the Six of Pentacles mean when we ask if our husband is cheating on us? This card represents charity, on the face of it, but what does it mean when we ask a specific question about an interpersonal relationship?)

Readers will come away from this book knowing how to interpret the Tarot cards in relation to specific topics within a love reading, such as love triangles, cheating, divorce, flirting, marriage, romantic interest, and communication issues.

Tarot can be a powerful tool for gaining insight and guidance in matters of love and relationships. Whether you are seeking answers about a current relationship, a potential romance, or trying to navigate through a difficult situation, Tarot can provide valuable discernment to help.

And so, without further ado, let's sit back, light some incense, and open up our minds – we're going to *finally* learn how to do love readings using our Tarot cards!

Structure of a Tarot Deck

I want to start by introducing you to the structure of a standard Tarot deck, as it is useful information for a beginner. If you already know the structure, you can skip this section, since there will likely not be too much information you don't already know here for you. If you've read my other book, "Quick and Dirty Tarot," this chapter will be very familiar to you!

A standard Tarot deck consists of 78 cards divided into two main categories: the Major Arcana and the Minor Arcana.

The Major Arcana consists of 22 cards that represent major life events and spiritual lessons. These cards are often referred to as the "trump cards" because they are seen as the most powerful and significant in the deck. Each Major Arcana card features a distinct image and a unique meaning, and they are often associated with specific archetypes, such as the Fool, the Magician, and the High Priestess, etc.

The Minor Arcana, on the other hand, consists of 56 cards divided into 4 suits: Wands, Cups, Swords, and Pentacles. Each suit represents a different aspect of life: Wands represent creativity, Cups represent emotions and relationships, Swords represent intellect and communication, and Pentacles represent material and financial matters. Each suit consists of 14 cards, including ten numbered cards (Ace through Ten) and four court cards (Page, Knight, Queen, and King).

While the structure of a Tarot deck may seem complex at first glance, it is actually quite simple once you understand the basic categories and, eventually, the meanings of each card.

The Major Arcana:

There are 22 Major Arcana cards, numbered 0 to 21 in Roman numerals at the top (usually) and with the name of the card at the bottom (usually). Here is a list of the Major Arcana cards if you want to see them listed in numerical order:

0 - The Fool
I - The Magician
II - The High Priestess
III - The Empress
IV - The Emperor
V - The Hierophant
VI - The Lovers
VII - The Chariot
VIII - Strength
IX - The Hermit
X - The Wheel of Fortune
XI - Justice
XII - The Hanged Man
XIII - Death
XIV - Temperance
XV - The Devil
XVI - The Tower
XVII - The Star
XVIII - The Moon
XIX - The Sun
XX - Judgment
XI - The World

These cards are generally weighted more heavily in a reading and are said to deal with more serious subjects like love, loss, family, or the big decisions we make in life. The Minor Arcana, on the other hand, deal more with the day-to-day goings on such as work, gossip, crushes, conversations, money exchange, travel, or feelings people have for us or that we have for them.

The Minor Arcana are 78 minus the 22 Major Arcana, leaving us with 56 cards. Those 56 cards are divided into 4 groups or suits: the Wands, the Swords, the Cups, and the Pentacles. There are 14 Wand cards, 14 Sword cards, 14 Cup cards, and 14 Pentacle cards.

Of each of these 14 cards, 4 of them in each suit are court cards. The court cards include the Pages (sometimes the Princesses), the Knights (sometimes the Princes), the Queens, and the Kings. So, we have 4 sets of 4 court cards representing each suit, leaving us with Pages, Knights, Queens and Kings of each suit: Page, Knight, Queen and King of Wands, of Swords, of Cups, and of Pentacles.

The Minor Arcana are divided numerically and are numbered Aces (representing the number 1) through 10, all, again, in Roman numerals, until you reach the court cards.

Now, looking at the general organization and structure of a Tarot deck, you might notice that some cards feature people more prominently (especially the Major Arcana and the Court Cards) and some don't. The cards that do feature people more prominently can represent people and feelings, or concepts in a reading, and more often than not, it *is* the case that a "person card" will actually represent a real person rather than just a concept, *however*, do keep in mind that people cards *can* also mean concepts.

This point can be confusing for new readers, especially when they run into the court cards, but knowing whether or not a person card really represents an actual person will require two things (1) the context of the question and situation and (2) your intuition - what are you leaning more towards? The card being a person or a concept? You'd be surprised at how often you will get this right based simply off of gut feeling - I know I was always surprised when I was just learning, and even now after years of practice, I still surprise myself at how accurate I can get my readings when I trust my gut.

Overall, in love readings, **the person cards are more often than not representative of actual people**, especially when they are court cards.

Choosing a Tarot Deck

There are thousands of beautiful Tarot decks out there on the market now, and I wouldn't blame anyone if they felt overwhelmed when looking at their options. These days, you can find any type of theme applied to the standard Tarot deck, and one of them is actually the theme of love and love interpretations!

I want to say right off the bat that there is no reason for you to purchase a Tarot deck that specifically caters to love interpretations unless you *want* to have such a deck! It is completely possible to do love readings with a standard Tarot deck, such as the Rider-Waite-Smith deck (from here on out called the RWS deck).

This book works exclusively with the RWS deck as it is a wonderful beginner deck, and also a deck which many other decks and artworks have been inspired by. This book's aim is not to have you use a shortcut by simply purchasing a love Tarot deck (which you are, of course, free to do!) but rather, to help you apply love interpretations to all the cards of the RWS Tarot, even when a particular card doesn't seem to be about love at all.

Again, I am not telling you not to purchase love Tarot decks, I'm saying you don't have to use such decks if you want to read Tarot for love questions! This book will teach you how to do that with the RWS deck, alone!

Cards that Represent Love

If you've ever seen a standard Tarot deck before, you'll probably agree with me that some cards very obviously pertain to love, while other cards look as though they have nothing to do with love at all. Take, for example, the Lovers card. There's no other card in the deck that is as obviously about love as this one, is there?

Although this card does represent love, marriage, partnerships, trysts, soul mates, and sexual attraction between two people, it also represents decisions in traditional Tarot literature. There are several reasons why the Lovers card is associated with decisions. First, the card depicts a man and a woman standing in front of an angel or a divine figure, often with their arms raised towards each other. This imagery suggests that the choice between two paths or options is being guided by a higher power or spiritual force.

Second, the Lovers card often appears in readings that focus on relationships or partnerships. In this context, the card can represent the need to choose between two potential romantic partners or to make a decision about the future of an existing relationship.

Finally, the Lovers card can also be interpreted as a symbol of duality, representing the choice between two opposing forces or ideas. This could include choices related to career, lifestyle, or personal values. So, you can see that this card, in particular, does represent love and relationships, but it is muddied up by some of the other more grandiose meanings, as it is a Major Arcana card.

One can argue that another card, the Two of Cups, is a better representation of love and relationships than the Lovers card, as it shows two people in a state of mutual giving and taking. Looking at the imagery of the Two of Cups, it should make sense to us that this card should remind us of love and relationships.

Here, we see two people in equal exchange with some entity above and between them, in similar fashion to the Lovers card. These two are looking at each other and interacting with one another, whereas in the Lover's card, the man is looking at the woman while the woman is looking up at the angel in the sky. In the Two of Cups, the floating lion head can represent the strength and courage needed to build and maintain a healthy and balanced relationship. The lion's mane is also reminiscent of a halo that extends over the heads of the two characters in the card, which could suggest a spiritual or divine element to the relationship (to say nothing of the laurel crowns they are both wearing that also look like halos!).

The caduceus, which is a symbol of the Greek god Hermes, consists of two intertwined snakes and a winged staff. The caduceus has various interpretations, but it is commonly associated with communication, balance, and healing. In the Two of Cups, the caduceus could represent the importance of communication and balance in a relationship. It could also suggest the potential for healing and growth that can come from a harmonious partnership.

These are just two of the best examples of cards that really exemplify the concept of love in the Tarot. You could know absolutely nothing about Tarot at all, see these two cards and immediately have an idea that the topic being expressed is related to love and relationships.

In addition to the Lovers and the Two of Cups, I would argue that the following list of cards also fairly obviously represent love in the Tarot:

1. The Ace of Cups: The Ace of Cups represents new beginnings in love and relationships, including emotional fulfillment, deep connections, and love overflowing.
2. The Ten of Cups: The Ten of Cups represents ultimate emotional fulfillment, joy, and harmony in a loving relationship or family.
3. The Four of Wands: The Four of Wands represents celebration, harmony, and stability within a romantic partnership.
4. The Knight of Cups: The Knight of Cups represents romantic gestures, emotional expression, and following your heart in matters of love.

5. The Queen of Cups: The Queen of Cups represents emotional intelligence, empathy, and nurturing love.
6. The King of Cups: The King of Cups represents emotional balance, wisdom, and mature love.
7. The Empress: The Empress represents motherly love, fertility, abundance, and nurturing in relationships.
8. The Emperor: The Emperor represents protection, stability, and structure within a loving relationship.
9. The Hierophant: The Hierophant represents commitment, tradition, and guidance within a loving relationship.
10. The Six of Cups: The Six of Cups represents nostalgia, innocence, and fond memories of past relationships.
11. The Nine of Cups: The Nine of Cups represents emotional satisfaction, wishes fulfilled, and happiness in love.
12. The Page of Cups: The Page of Cups represents emotional messages, creative expression, and new emotional experiences in love.
13. The Three of Cups: The Three of Cups represents joyous celebration, community, and friendship in relationships.
14. The Five of Cups: The Five of Cups represents loss, grief, and emotional pain in relationships.
15. The Eight of Cups: The Eight of Cups represents moving on from emotional pain and seeking emotional fulfillment elsewhere.
16. The Ten of Pentacles: The Ten of Pentacles represents familial love, financial stability, and the legacy of love passed down through generations.
17. The Four of Swords: The Four of Swords represents taking time to heal and recover from emotional pain in relationships.
18. The Justice card: The Justice card represents fairness, balance, and equality in relationships and can indicate the need for compromise, communication, and mutual respect.
19. The Three of Swords: The Three of Swords represents heartbreak, betrayal, and emotional pain in love and relationships. Its imagery and numerology may suggest a "love triangle," or the heartbreak that comes with infidelity.

20. The Tower: The Tower card is often associated with sudden upheaval or change. It can represent the end of a relationship or the need for significant changes within a current relationship.
21. The Devil: The Devil card is the mirrored shadow of the Lovers card and represents toxic relationships, codependency, and external forces that bind two people together such as addiction, stalking, domestic violence, or contractual obligations.

These are really just my suggestions to get you started thinking about how the Tarot can answer your questions about love and relationships. If you go through your own tarot deck, I urge you to spend some time with the images and pick out the cards that remind *you* of love, romance, and relationships. You might find that you have a different list than the one I just gave you - however, I'm sure there will be a good bit of overlap!

A quick note about the suit of Cups: The Cups in the Tarot are often associated with emotions, feelings, intuition, and creativity, more than any other suit. The Cups represent the element of water, which is connected to the realm of feelings and the unconscious mind. As a result, the Cups cards are often used to explore matters of the heart, including love, romance, and relationships.

The imagery and symbolism of the Cups cards often depict emotional connections between people, intimacy, and the many facets of human emotion that are involved in romantic relationships. This is why the list I just gave you above is so Cup-heavy. You might find that your own list will also be Cup-heavy, but it doesn't have to be!

In any event, I suggest you do this exercise in order to familiarize yourself with the cards that will be the most obvious to you when asking about love and romance. Once you have that list and can connect to it, you can slowly integrate more cards that are less obviously about love into your repertoire. For example, the least love-like cards would be in the suit of Pentacles, which is often associated with money, career, and finance. As we will see throughout this book, however, even these cards have their love meanings! Once you master these less obvious cards, you will never have trouble doing love readings for yourself or for others ever again!

Reversed Cards

A reversed card occurs when a card shows up in your reading upside down. Sometimes it happens by accident when you shuffle, but some people do it on purpose by mixing their cards in such a way as to cause reversals to happen. I personally do read reversed cards, but it's a matter of personal preference whether you want to or not. This book will provide reversed card meanings, but you don't have to follow them or accept them at all.

To me, reversed cards are an important aspect of Tarot readings, providing a layer of nuance and complexity to the interpretation of the cards. When a Tarot card is drawn in a reading and appears upside down, or reversed, it can indicate a different meaning than when the card appears upright.

The use of reversals in Tarot readings adds depth to the interpretation of the cards, providing a more robust understanding of the situation being examined. Reversals can also highlight areas of shadow or challenge that may be present, inviting the querent to explore these aspects more deeply.

In a Tarot reading, a reversed card can represent a block or obstacle that needs to be overcome, or an area of the querent's life that may be out of balance. For example, a reversed card in a love reading may suggest that there are underlying issues or challenges in the relationship that need to be addressed before the relationship can move forward.

It's important to note, again, that not all Tarot readers use reversals in their readings, but I do! Some readers prefer to focus solely on the upright meanings of the cards, while others may use reversals selectively, depending on the context of the reading.

Whether or not to use reversals in a Tarot reading ultimately comes down to personal preference and style. It's important for you to experiment and find the approach that works best for you and your clients.

It's also worth noting that when interpreting reversed cards, it's important to take into account the context of the reading and the other cards that are present. A reversed card on its own may indicate one thing, but when viewed in the context of the other cards in the spread, its meaning may shift or become more complex.

Ultimately, I feel reversed cards are an important aspect of Tarot readings, providing additional layers of meaning and depth to the interpretation of the cards, but whether or not you choose to use reversals in your Tarot readings is a matter of personal preference. Further, when interpreting reversed cards, it's important to consider the context of the reading and the other cards present in the spread, if you choose to use them.

Meanings of the Major Arcana

As we are about to find out, all of the cards in the Tarot deck have the potential to offer valuable insights into love and relationships, however, none are more significant than the Major Arcana.

The 22 cards of the Major Arcana represent major life events and spiritual lessons, and they can offer profound insights into the complexities of love, romance, and relationships. These cards aid us in interpreting the feelings and motivations of both parties in a partnership. They can provide clues to unresolved issues that may be hindering the success of a relationship, as well as insight into the potential outcome of a current or future situation.

The Major Arcana can also be used to help a person make big decisions about love, such as when to commit to a relationship, how to end a relationship, or when to seek outside help. By providing insight into the possible consequences of a particular decision, the Trump cards, as they are also called, can help us make the most informed choice possible.

Finally, cards of the Major Arcana can also be used as a tool to gain a better understanding of ourselves. By reflecting on the cards' interpretations, we can gain insight into our own behavior and motivations in the context of our relationships. This can help us be more aware of our actions and make better decisions when it comes to love.

From the Fool to the World, in this chapter, we will delve into the meaning of each card, focusing on the romantic aspects of those meanings and draw up guidance and insight into the many facets of love and relationships.

So let's begin our journey into the heart of the Tarot and discover the love meanings of the Major Arcana, starting with the Fool!

The Fool

In matters of love and relationships, the Fool card in the upright position suggests that you are embarking on a new adventure with a sense of innocence and enthusiasm. You are eager to take risks and explore new possibilities in your love life. This can indicate the beginning of a new relationship, or a renewal of passion in an existing one. You may be feeling free-spirited and unencumbered, ready to take a leap of faith and trust in the unknown. For those asking about an ex partner, this card indicates that the person in question is ready to try to rekindle the relationship once again, starting afresh.

> A new relationship or phase of an existing relationship is on the horizon.
> You are ready to take risks and embrace new experiences in your love life.
> Trust your instincts and intuition when it comes to matters of the heart.
> Be open to unexpected opportunities and surprises in your love life.
> Don't be afraid to take a chance on love.
> An ex lover is interested in rekindling the romance.

The Fool card in the reversed position suggests that you may be feeling stuck or hesitant to take action. You may be holding back due to fear or uncertainty, or you may be feeling overwhelmed by the risks involved in pursuing a new relationship. It's possible that you may be making impulsive decisions or acting recklessly in your love life, which could lead to negative consequences. For those asking about an ex, this card indicates that a second chance for the relationship seems unlikely or useless.

> You may be holding back or hesitating in matters of the heart.
> Be careful of impulsive decisions or reckless behavior in your love life.
> You may be feeling overwhelmed by the risks involved in pursuing a new relationship.

Don't rush into anything without careful consideration of the
potential consequences.
Take time to reflect on your desires and motivations in your
love life.
An ex does not feel a new start is possible for an old
relationship.

The Magician

The Magician card in the upright position suggests that you have the
power to manifest your desires and create the relationship you want.
You have the ability to communicate effectively and use your charm
and charisma to attract a partner who shares your values and goals.
You may also be feeling confident and in control of your love life, able
to take action and make things happen.

> You have the power to manifest the relationship you desire.
> Your communication skills and charm are an asset in your love
> life.
> You are in control of your love life and able to take action.
> Trust your instincts and use your intuition to guide your
> decisions in matters of the heart.

The Magician card in the reversed position suggests that you may be
experiencing a lack of clarity or direction. You may be feeling unsure of
your desires or how to communicate effectively with your partner. It's
possible that you may be using manipulation or deceit to get what you
want, which can ultimately lead to negative consequences in your love
life. In turn, someone may be using deceit to get what they want from
you in a relationship.

> You may be experiencing a lack of clarity or direction in your
> love life.
> Be honest and clear in your communication with your partner.
> Avoid using manipulation or deceit to get what you want in your
> relationships.
> Take time to reflect on your values and goals in your love life.

Seek guidance and support from trusted friends or a counselor
to help you navigate any challenges in your relationships.
Be mindful of any manipulation or deceit in your relationships.

<u>The High Priestess</u>

The High Priestess card in the upright position suggests that you
should trust your intuition and pay attention to your inner voice. You
may be going through a period of introspection, exploring your own
desires and needs in a relationship. This card can indicate the
importance of maintaining emotional boundaries and listening to your
gut instincts when it comes to matters of the heart. This card also
suggests to hold back on expressing yourself too openly, or confessing
too much at this time.

> Trust your intuition and inner voice when it comes to matters of
> the heart.
> Take time for introspection and self-reflection to explore your
> own desires and needs in a relationship.
> Maintain emotional boundaries and listen to your gut instincts
> in your relationships.
> Be open to receiving guidance from a trusted source or mentor.
> Pay attention to subtle signs and symbols in your love life.

The High Priestess card in the reversed position suggests that you
may be ignoring your intuition or disregarding your inner voice. You
may be struggling to connect with your own desires or may be
experiencing a lack of clarity in your love life. This card can indicate
the importance of listening to your emotions and paying attention to
the energy of the people around you. It may also suggest that now is a
good time to get things off your chest, especially if you have been
keeping your feelings or thoughts a secret from your partner.

> Pay attention to your emotions and listen to your intuition when
> it comes to matters of the heart.
> Connect with your own desires and needs in a relationship.

Be wary of ignoring your intuition or disregarding your inner
voice.
Seek guidance from a trusted source or mentor to help you
navigate any challenges in your relationships.
Pay attention to the energy and intentions of the people around
you in your love life.

<u>The Empress</u>

The Empress card in the upright position suggests that you are
experiencing a period of abundance and fertility. This card can indicate
the presence of nurturing and loving energy in your relationships, and
a deep connection with the natural world. You may be feeling
supported and cared for by your partner, or you may be embodying
these qualities yourself, bringing love and support to your relationship.

> You are experiencing a period of abundance and fertility in your
> love life.
> Your relationships are nurtured by loving and supportive
> energy.
> You may be feeling supported and cared for by your partner.
> You are embodying nurturing and loving qualities in your
> relationship.
> You have a deep connection with the natural world, and this
> may influence your relationships.

The Empress card in the reversed position suggests that you may be
experiencing a lack of nurturing or support in your relationships. You
may be feeling disconnected from your partner or struggling to express
your emotions in a meaningful way. This card can also indicate a need
for self-care and self-love, as you may be neglecting your own needs
in your relationships.

> You may be experiencing a lack of nurturing or support in your
> relationships.
> You may be feeling disconnected from your partner or
> struggling to express your emotions.

You need to focus on self-care and self-love to nourish your relationships.
You may be neglecting your own needs in your relationships.
You may be experiencing challenges with fertility or conception.

The Emperor

The Emperor card in the upright position represents stability, structure, and commitment. This card suggests a need for a strong and steady foundation in a relationship, built on trust, respect, and loyalty. It can indicate a desire for a partner who embodies the qualities of leadership, protection, and guidance, someone who can provide a sense of security and order in the relationship. It can also indicate the presence of stability and structure in your relationship, as well as a need for clear communication and boundaries. You may be feeling confident and in control, or you may be drawn to partners who exhibit these qualities.

You are embodying leadership and authority in your relationship.
Your relationship is characterized by stability and structure.
Traditional approach to relationships with an emphasis on family and responsibility.
Clear communication and boundaries are important for a healthy relationship.
You may be feeling confident and in control in your love life.
You may be drawn to partners who exhibit leadership and authority qualities.

The Emperor card in the reversed position suggests that you may be struggling with issues related to control or authority. You may be experiencing a power struggle in your relationship or feeling like your boundaries are not being respected. This card can indicate a tendency to be controlling or domineering in the relationship, or a difficulty in establishing clear boundaries and roles. It may also suggest a lack of discipline or self-control, leading to instability or chaos in the relationship. This card can also indicate a need to let go of rigid structures or expectations and embrace more flexibility and openness in your relationships. The reversed Emperor card can also suggest a need for greater emotional expression and vulnerability in the relationship, as well as a need to break free from traditional or restrictive roles and explore new possibilities in the relationship.

> You may be struggling with issues related to control or authority in your relationships.
> You may be experiencing a power struggle with your partner or feeling like your boundaries are not being respected.
> Tendency to be controlling or domineering in the relationship.
> You may need to let go of rigid structures or expectations in your relationships.
> Lack of structure, stability, and commitment.
> Embracing more flexibility and openness may be necessary for a healthy relationship.
> You may be experiencing challenges with establishing clear communication in your relationship.

The Hierophant

The Hierophant card in the upright position represents a deep commitment to tradition, stability, and structure. This card can indicate a long-term relationship or marriage, as well as a strong spiritual or religious bond with your partner. You may be seeking guidance or advice from a trusted source, such as a religious or spiritual leader, in order to strengthen your relationship.

> You are committed to tradition and stability in your romantic life.
> Your relationship is based on strong spiritual or religious principles.
> You may be seeking guidance or advice from a trusted source in order to strengthen your relationship.
> You may be embarking on a long-term relationship or marriage.
> Your relationship is grounded in a deep sense of commitment and structure.

The Hierophant card in the reversed position suggests a lack of structure and stability. This card can indicate a time of rebellion against traditional values or expectations, which may lead to conflict or confusion in your relationship. You may be struggling to find common ground with your partner, or feeling disillusioned with the ideals and beliefs that once guided your relationship.

> You may be experiencing a period of rebellion against traditional values in your romantic life.
> Your relationship may lack structure and stability.
> You may be struggling to find common ground with your partner.
> You may be feeling disillusioned with the ideals and beliefs that once guided your relationship.
> You may need to re-examine your values and beliefs in order to move forward in your romantic life.

The Lovers

The Lovers card in the upright position represents the union of two individuals who share a strong emotional and spiritual connection. This card can indicate a new romantic relationship, or the deepening of an existing one. You may be experiencing a period of harmony and balance in your relationship, and are open to exploring new possibilities and deepening your connection with your partner.

> You are entering into a powerful romantic relationship.
> Your relationship is based on mutual respect, trust, and love.
> You are experiencing a deep emotional and spiritual connection with your partner.
> You are open to exploring new possibilities and deepening your connection with your partner.
> Your current relationship is harmonious and balanced.

The Lovers card in the reversed position suggests that there may be a lack of harmony and balance in your relationship. This card can indicate a period of indecision, or a time when you may be questioning the authenticity of your connection with your partner. You may be struggling with a decision regarding your relationship, or feeling a sense of disharmony and imbalance.

> You may be experiencing a challenging period in your romantic relationship.
> There may be a lack of harmony and balance in your current relationship.
> You may be questioning the authenticity of your connection with your partner.
> You may be facing a difficult decision regarding your relationship.
> You may need to re-evaluate your priorities in your romantic life.

The Chariot

The Chariot card in the upright position suggests a period of forward momentum and triumph. This card can indicate that you have overcome obstacles in your relationship or that you are ready to take charge and move forward with confidence. You may be feeling a sense of motivation and determination in your relationship, and may need to take action to achieve your goals.

> You are experiencing a period of forward momentum and triumph in your romantic life.
> You may have overcome obstacles in your relationship or are ready to take charge and move forward with confidence.
> You may be feeling a sense of motivation and determination in your relationship and may need to take action to achieve your goals.
> Your relationship is on the right track and is moving in a positive direction.
> You are being called to be assertive and take control of your romantic life.

The Chariot card in the reversed position suggests a lack of direction and control. This card can indicate that you are feeling stuck or unable to move forward in your relationship. You may be experiencing a sense of frustration or impatience and may need to reassess your goals and priorities in order to move forward.

> You may be feeling a lack of direction and control in your romantic life.
> You may be feeling stuck or unable to move forward in your relationship.
> You may be experiencing a sense of frustration or impatience and may need to reassess your goals and priorities in order to move forward.
> Your relationship may be going through a period of stagnation or lack of progress.
> You are being called to let go of control and surrender to the flow of your romantic life.

Strength

The Strength card in the upright position suggests a need for patience, compassion, and understanding. This card can indicate that you are being called to approach your relationship with a gentle and caring touch, rather than with force or aggression. You may need to exercise self-control and find inner strength to overcome any challenges that arise in your relationship.

> You are being called to approach your relationship with patience, compassion, and understanding.
> You may need to exercise self-control and find inner strength to overcome any challenges that arise in your relationship.
> You have the power to bring balance and harmony to your romantic life.
> Your relationship may require a nurturing touch in order to grow and flourish.
> Your love life may be going through a period of emotional transformation and growth.

The Strength card in the reversed position suggests a lack of inner strength and self-control. This card can indicate that you may be feeling overwhelmed or out of control in your relationship, and may need to take a step back and reassess the situation. You may be struggling to find the balance and harmony that is needed for a healthy relationship.

> You may be feeling a lack of inner strength and self-control in your romantic life.
> You may be feeling overwhelmed or out of control in your relationship, and may need to take a step back and reassess the situation.
> Your relationship may be out of balance or lacking in harmony. You may need to exercise more patience, compassion, and understanding in order to improve your relationship.
> You may be feeling drained or depleted, and need to take time to recharge and regain your strength.

The Hermit

The Hermit card in the upright position suggests a need for introspection and solitude. This card can indicate a time of reflection and self-discovery, where you may need to withdraw from social activities and focus on your inner self. You may be seeking guidance or wisdom from a trusted source, such as a mentor or spiritual guide, in order to gain a deeper understanding of yourself and your relationship.

> You are in a period of introspection and self-discovery in your romantic life.
> You may need to withdraw from social activities and focus on your inner self.
> You may be seeking guidance or wisdom from a trusted source in order to gain a deeper understanding of yourself and your relationship.

You may need to take time alone to reflect on your relationship and your role in it.
You are being called to embrace your inner wisdom and intuition in your romantic life.

The Hermit card in the reversed position suggests a reluctance to seek guidance or advice. This card can indicate a time of isolation or feeling lost, where you may be struggling to find direction in your relationship. You may need to open yourself up to the support and advice of others in order to gain clarity and direction.

You may be reluctant to seek guidance or advice in your romantic life.
You may be feeling lost or isolated in your relationship.
You may need to open yourself up to the support and advice of others in order to gain clarity and direction.
You may need to overcome your fear of vulnerability in order to move forward in your romantic life.
You are being called to embrace the support and guidance of others in your romantic life.

The Wheel of Fortune

In matters of love and relationships, the Wheel of Fortune card in the upright position suggests that you are in a period of transition or change. This card can indicate that your relationship may be going through a major shift or turning point, and you need to be open and adaptable to these changes. This card can also suggest that your relationship is experiencing a stroke of luck or positive change, so be open to new opportunities and possibilities.

Your relationship may be going through a major shift or turning point.
You need to be open and adaptable to the changes that are occurring in your romantic life.
Your relationship is experiencing a stroke of luck or positive change, so be open to new opportunities and possibilities.

You may need to take a chance or make a bold move in order
to bring about positive change in your love life.
Your romantic future is looking bright and full of possibilities.

The Wheel of Fortune card in the reversed position suggests that you
may be experiencing a period of stagnation or a lack of progress in
your relationship. This card can indicate that you may be stuck in a
cycle of negative patterns or habits, and need to make a change in
order to move forward. This card can also suggest that you may be
resisting change or opportunities that could bring positive growth to
your relationship.

You may be experiencing a period of stagnation or a lack of
progress in your romantic life.
You may be stuck in a cycle of negative patterns or habits, and
need to make a change in order to move forward.
You may be resisting change or opportunities that could bring
positive growth to your relationship.
Your relationship may be going through a difficult period, but
know that it will pass and things will eventually turn around.
You may need to let go of control and allow the universe to
guide you towards positive change in your love life.

Justice

The Justice card in the upright position suggests that there may be a
need for balance and fairness in your romantic life. This card can
indicate that you or your partner may be seeking justice or fairness in
the relationship, and it is important to have open communication and
honesty in order to achieve this. This card can also suggest that legal
or contractual matters may be influencing your relationship, and it is
important to have a fair and just resolution.

There may be a need for balance and fairness in your romantic
life.
You or your partner may be seeking justice or fairness in the
relationship.

It is important to have open communication and honesty in order to achieve balance and fairness.
Legal or contractual matters may be influencing your relationship, and it is important to have a fair and just resolution.
Justice will prevail in your romantic life.

The Justice card in the reversed position suggests that there may be a lack of balance or fairness in your romantic life. This card can indicate that you or your partner may be behaving unfairly or unjustly in the relationship, and it is important to take responsibility for your actions and make amends. This card can also suggest that legal or contractual matters may not be resolved fairly, and it is important to seek legal counsel if necessary. When asking about a breakup, this card may indicate a divorce - a separation that involves the courts.

There may be a lack of balance or fairness in your romantic life.
You or your partner may be behaving unfairly or unjustly in the relationship, and it is important to take responsibility for your actions and make amends.
Legal or contractual matters may not be resolved fairly, and it is important to seek legal counsel if necessary.
You may need to make a sacrifice in order to restore balance and fairness in your relationship.
Justice may be delayed, but it will eventually prevail.

<u>Hanged Man</u>

The Hanged Man card in the upright position suggests a need to approach your romantic life from a different perspective. This card can indicate that you may need to sacrifice or let go of certain beliefs or attitudes that are no longer serving you in order to move forward in your relationship. This card can also suggest a need for patience and surrender in your romantic life, and it is important to trust the process and allow things to unfold naturally.

A need to approach your romantic life from a different perspective.
You may need to sacrifice or let go of certain beliefs or attitudes that are no longer serving you in order to move forward in your relationship.
A need for patience and surrender in your romantic life.
Trust the process and allow things to unfold naturally.
A sacrifice in the present may lead to greater rewards in the future.

The Hanged Man card in the reversed position suggests a resistance to change or a lack of willingness to let go of old patterns or beliefs that may be holding you back in your relationship. This card can indicate a need to let go of control and trust in the process of your romantic life, and it is important to be open to new perspectives and possibilities. This card can also suggest that you may be feeling stuck or stagnant in your relationship, and it is important to take action in order to move forward.

Resistance to change or a lack of willingness to let go of old patterns or beliefs.
A need to let go of control and trust in the process of your romantic life.
Be open to new perspectives and possibilities.
Feeling stuck or stagnant in your relationship, and it is important to take action in order to move forward.
A sacrifice may be required in order to break free from old patterns or beliefs.

Death

The Death card in the upright position suggests a significant transformation or change that is necessary in your romantic life. This card can indicate the end of a current relationship or the need to let go of old patterns and beliefs in order to move forward in your love life. However, this transformation can lead to new beginnings and opportunities in your romantic life, and it is important to embrace the change with an open mind and heart. When asking about a breakup, this card is usually representative of an end or separation.

> A significant transformation or change is necessary in your romantic life.
> The end of a current relationship or the need to let go of old patterns and beliefs in order to move forward in your love life. Embrace the change with an open mind and heart.
> A new beginning or opportunity may arise from this transformation.
> This card can also represent a need to face your fears or confront difficult emotions in order to move forward in your romantic life.

The Death card in the reversed position suggests a resistance to change or a fear of letting go of the past. This card can indicate a need to release old patterns and beliefs that are no longer serving you in order to move forward in your romantic life. It is important to let go of what is holding you back and embrace new beginnings and opportunities in your love life.

> Resistance to change or a fear of letting go of the past.
> A need to release old patterns and beliefs that are no longer serving you in your romantic life.
> Let go of what is holding you back and embrace new beginnings and opportunities in your love life.
> A fear of transformation or change in your romantic life.
> This card can also represent a need to confront difficult emotions or face your fears in order to move forward in your love life.

<u>Temperance</u>

The Temperance card in the upright position suggests finding balance and harmony in your romantic life. This card can indicate the need to take a patient and moderate approach to your relationships, and to work towards creating a harmonious partnership with your significant other. It is important to communicate openly and listen to your partner's needs in order to create a healthy and balanced relationship.

> Finding balance and harmony in your romantic life.
> A patient and moderate approach to your relationships.
> Working towards creating a harmonious partnership with your significant other.
> Communication and listening are key to creating a healthy and balanced relationship.
> This card can also indicate a need to find inner peace and balance within yourself in order to attract a healthy and balanced relationship.

The Temperance card in the reversed position suggests a lack of balance and harmony in your romantic life. This card can indicate a need to take a step back and reevaluate your relationships, as well as your own behavior and patterns within them. It is important to find a middle ground and compromise in order to create a healthy and balanced relationship.

> A lack of balance and harmony in your romantic life.
> A need to take a step back and reevaluate your relationships.
> Finding a middle ground and compromising to create a healthy and balanced relationship.
> This card can also indicate a need to let go of unhealthy patterns and behaviors in order to create a healthier and more balanced relationship.
> It is important to find inner peace and balance within yourself before you can create a healthy and balanced relationship with a partner.

The Devil

The Devil card in the upright position suggests a strong physical attraction or addiction to a person or situation. This card can indicate a need to be aware of any unhealthy or toxic behaviors in your relationships, and to work towards breaking free from any negative patterns or cycles. It is important to take responsibility for your actions and to communicate openly with your partner in order to create a healthy and balanced relationship. This card can also indicate a need to be aware of any power imbalances in your relationships, and to work towards creating a more equal partnership.

A strong physical attraction or addiction to a person or situation.
Being aware of any unhealthy or toxic behaviors in your relationships.
Breaking free from negative patterns or cycles.
Taking responsibility for your actions and communicating openly with your partner to create a healthy and balanced relationship.

The Devil card in the reversed position suggests a release from any unhealthy or toxic relationships or patterns. This card can indicate a need to let go of any negative attachments or dependencies in your relationships, and to work towards finding inner freedom and self-love. It is important to take a step back and evaluate your relationships and behaviors in order to create a healthy and balanced relationship. This card can also indicate a need to be aware of any temptations or negative influences in your relationships, and to resist any urges to engage in unhealthy or destructive behaviors.

Release from any unhealthy or toxic relationships or patterns.
Letting go of negative attachments or dependencies in your relationships.
Finding inner freedom and self-love.
Taking a step back and evaluating your relationships and behaviors in order to create a healthy and balanced relationship.

The Tower

The Tower card in the upright position suggests a sudden and unexpected upheaval or change. This card can indicate a need to let go of any illusions or false beliefs about your relationships and to be open to transformation and growth. It may be a challenging and difficult time, but it can also bring a breakthrough or a new beginning. It is important to embrace the change and to trust in the process, even if it feels uncomfortable or uncertain.

A sudden and unexpected upheaval or change in your relationships.
Letting go of illusions or false beliefs about your relationships.
Being open to transformation and growth.
Embracing the change and trusting in the process, even if it feels uncomfortable or uncertain.
This card can also indicate a need to be honest and truthful with yourself and your partner, and to communicate openly and directly in order to move forward.

The Tower card in the reversed position suggests a resistance to change or a fear of letting go of old patterns or beliefs. This card can indicate a need to release any resistance and to embrace the process of transformation and growth. It may be a time of uncertainty and instability, but it can also bring new opportunities and growth. It is important to trust in the process and to be open to new experiences.

Resistance to change or a fear of letting go of old patterns or beliefs.
Releasing resistance and embracing the process of transformation and growth.
A time of uncertainty and instability that can bring new opportunities and growth.
Trusting in the process and being open to new experiences.
This card can also indicate a need to be patient and to take things slow in order to avoid any unnecessary upheaval or chaos.

The Star

The Star card in the upright position suggests a time of hope and inspiration. This card can indicate a renewal of faith in yourself and in your relationships, and a sense of clarity and guidance in your path towards love. It is important to remain optimistic and open to new experiences and connections.

> A time of hope and inspiration.
> Renewal of faith in yourself and in your relationships.
> Clarity and guidance in your path towards love.
> Remaining optimistic and open to new experiences and connections.
> This card can also indicate a need to be aware of any unrealistic expectations or ideals in your relationships, and to focus on finding balance and harmony.

The Star card in the reversed position suggests a time of disillusionment or loss of faith. This card can indicate a need to release any unrealistic expectations or attachments in your relationships, and to focus on finding inner peace and healing. It is important to take time for self-care and to be patient with yourself as you navigate through difficult emotions.

> Disillusionment or loss of faith.
> Releasing unrealistic expectations or attachments in your relationships.
> Finding inner peace and healing.
> Taking time for self-care and being patient with yourself as you navigate through difficult emotions.
> This card can also indicate a need to be aware of any fears or doubts that may be holding you back in your relationships, and to work towards overcoming them with self-love and self-acceptance.

The Moon

The Moon card in the upright position suggests a time of uncertainty and confusion. This card can indicate that you may be experiencing emotional ups and downs or feeling lost in your relationship. It is important to trust your intuition and be aware of any hidden emotions or intentions in your relationships. This card also urges you to communicate openly with your partner and seek clarity in your feelings.

Uncertainty and confusion.
Emotional ups and downs or feeling lost in your relationship.
Trusting your intuition and being aware of any hidden emotions or intentions in your relationships.
Communicating openly with your partner and seeking clarity in your feelings.
This card can also indicate a need to be aware of any illusions or deceptions in your relationships, and to seek the truth in order to move forward.

The Moon card in the reversed position suggests a time of clarity and resolution. This card can indicate that you are overcoming any confusion or uncertainty in your relationship, and that you may have gained a deeper understanding of your emotions and needs. It is important to trust your intuition and take action towards positive change in your relationships.

Clarity and resolution.
Overcoming confusion or uncertainty in your relationship.
Gaining a deeper understanding of your emotions and needs.
Trusting your intuition and taking action towards positive change in your relationships.
This card can also indicate a need to be aware of any lingering fears or anxieties that may be holding you back in your relationships, and to work towards overcoming them with courage and self-love.

The Sun

The Sun card in the upright position suggests a time of joy and happiness. This card can indicate a harmonious and fulfilling relationship, where both partners are enjoying each other's company and basking in the warmth of love. It is a time for celebration and appreciation of the positive aspects of your relationship. This card also encourages you to share your happiness with others and spread positivity wherever you go.

Joy and happiness.
Harmonious and fulfilling relationship.
Celebration and appreciation of the positive aspects of your relationship.
Sharing your happiness with others and spreading positivity.
This card can also indicate a need to be aware of any tendencies towards being overly optimistic in your relationships, and to avoid ignoring any potential problems or red flags.

The Sun card in the reversed position suggests a time of challenges and setbacks. This card can indicate that your relationship is going through a difficult period, and that you may be facing obstacles or conflicts. It is important to remain optimistic and focused on finding solutions to the problems in your relationship. This card also urges you to communicate openly with your partner and to work together to overcome any issues.

Challenges and setbacks.
Difficult period in your relationship.
Facing obstacles or conflicts.
Remaining optimistic and focused on finding solutions.
This card can also indicate a need to be aware of any issues with ego or self-centeredness in your relationships, and to work towards being more selfless and understanding towards your partner's needs.

Judgment

In matters of love and relationships, the Judgment card in the upright position suggests a time of renewal and transformation. This card can indicate that you and your partner are going through a significant change in your relationship, such as a deepening of commitment or a fresh start. It is a time to let go of the past and move forward with a new perspective. This card also encourages you to be honest with yourself and your partner, and to take responsibility for your actions in order to create a healthier relationship.

> Renewal and transformation.
> Significant change in your relationship.
> Letting go of the past and moving forward with a new perspective.
> Being honest with yourself and your partner, and taking responsibility for your actions to create a healthier relationship.
> This card can also indicate a need to be aware of any feelings of guilt or regret in your relationships, and to work towards forgiveness and reconciliation.

The Judgment card in the reversed position suggests a time of resistance and reluctance. This card can indicate that you or your partner are hesitant to move forward in your relationship, perhaps due to fear or insecurity. It is important to address any underlying issues and to work through them in order to create a stronger relationship. This card also urges you to be open to change and to let go of any patterns or behaviors that are holding you back.

> Resistance and reluctance.
> Hesitation to move forward in your relationship.
> Addressing underlying issues and working through them to create a stronger relationship.
> Being open to change and letting go of patterns or behaviors that are holding you back.
> This card can also indicate a need to be aware of any feelings of self-doubt or indecisiveness in your relationships, and to work towards gaining clarity and confidence in your decisions.

The World

The World card in the upright position suggests a sense of completion and fulfillment. This card can indicate that you and your partner have reached a significant milestone in your relationship, such as a deepening of commitment or a sense of unity. It is a time to celebrate your achievements and to feel a sense of contentment and satisfaction. This card also encourages you to be open to new experiences and to continue growing together in your relationship.

> Completion and fulfillment.
> Reaching a significant milestone in your relationship.
> Celebrating your achievements and feeling a sense of contentment and satisfaction.
> Being open to new experiences and continuing to grow together in your relationship.
> This card can also indicate a need to be aware of any feelings of complacency in your relationship, and to continue putting effort into maintaining a strong and healthy partnership.

The World card in the reversed position suggests a sense of unfulfillment and unfinished business. This card can indicate that you or your partner are feeling a sense of dissatisfaction in your relationship, and that there is work to be done in order to achieve a sense of completion. It is important to address any issues or challenges in your relationship and to work towards resolution. This card also encourages you to be open to new possibilities and to continue striving for growth and improvement in your relationship.

> Unfulfillment and unfinished business.
> Feeling a sense of dissatisfaction in your relationship.
> Addressing issues or challenges in your relationship and working towards resolution.
> Being open to new possibilities and continuing to strive for growth and improvement in your relationship.
> This card can also indicate a need to be aware of any feelings of stagnation or resistance to change in your relationship, and to work towards breaking free from any negative patterns or cycles.

Meanings of the Minor Arcana: Wands

The suit of Wands in the Tarot is closely associated with passion, creativity, and inspiration. As such, it can be viewed as a symbol of the dynamic energy that drives interpersonal relationships, including love, romance, communication, and marriage. At the same time, the Wands can also be interpreted as a representation of the struggles and challenges that can arise in these relationships, including breakups and divorce.

One of the primary ways in which the Wands relates to love and romance is through its association with passion and desire. Just as the Wands are a symbol of creative energy, so too are they symbols of the intense emotions that often accompany romantic relationships. Whether it is the initial rush of attraction or the deep bond that develops over time, the Wands can represent the powerful force that draws people together and sustains their connection.

However, the Wands can also represent the challenges that arise in romantic relationships. Just as creativity and inspiration can be fleeting, so too can the intensity of passion and desire. When this energy wanes or fades, relationships can become strained or even fall apart altogether. In this way, the Wands can be a symbol of the difficult decisions and painful emotions that can accompany breakups and divorce.

Wands can also represent the ways in which communication and creativity can help to sustain and strengthen relationships. By fostering open and honest communication, couples can work through their problems and find ways to rekindle the passion and connection that initially drew them together. Similarly, by engaging in creative pursuits together, couples can find new ways to express their love and deepen their bond.

Whether it is through passion and desire, communication and creativity, or the ongoing effort required to sustain a marriage, the wand can serve as a reminder of the complexity and beauty of romantic interpersonal relationships.

Let us now dive into the divinatory meanings of the Wands as they relate to love and relationships!

<u>Ace of Wands</u>

In matters of love and relationships, the Ace of Wands in the upright position often indicates a new and passionate beginning, with a strong spark of attraction and desire. This card suggests a burst of creative energy and enthusiasm, as well as a willingness to take risks and pursue exciting opportunities. It may indicate a strong physical and sexual attraction, as well as a desire for adventure and spontaneity in relationships. This card can also suggest a need for clear communication and honest expression of desires, in order to establish mutual trust and understanding.

> New and passionate beginning with a strong spark of attraction and desire.
> Burst of creative energy and enthusiasm, and willingness to take risks and pursue exciting opportunities.
> Strong physical and sexual attraction, and desire for adventure and spontaneity in relationships.
> Need for clear communication and honest expression of desires to establish mutual trust and understanding.

The Ace of Wands in the reversed position suggests a need to slow down and reflect before taking action. This card can indicate a lack of direction or motivation, as well as a tendency towards impulsiveness or recklessness in relationships. It may also suggest a need to clarify one's own desires and values, in order to avoid confusion or misunderstandings in relationships. This card can also suggest a need to cultivate patience and self-discipline, in order to build a strong foundation for a lasting and fulfilling relationship.

> Need to slow down and reflect before taking action.

Lack of direction or motivation, and tendency towards
impulsiveness or recklessness in relationships.
Need to clarify one's own desires and values to avoid
confusion or misunderstandings in relationships.
Need to cultivate patience and self-discipline to build a strong
foundation for a lasting and fulfilling relationship.

<u>Two of Wands</u>

The Two of Wands in the upright position often indicates a period of
anticipation and planning for the future, with a focus on growth and
expansion. This card suggests a sense of ambition and confidence in
one's ability to create a fulfilling and exciting future with a partner. It
may indicate a desire for new experiences and a willingness to take
risks in order to achieve one's goals. This card can also suggest a
need for clear communication and collaboration in order to build a
strong and balanced partnership.

Anticipation and planning for the future with a focus on growth
and expansion.
Sense of ambition and confidence in one's ability to create a
fulfilling and exciting future with a partner.
Desire for new experiences and willingness to take risks to
achieve one's goals.
Need for clear communication and collaboration to build a
strong and balanced partnership.

The Two of Wands in the reversed position suggests a need to
re-evaluate one's plans and goals, and to consider alternative paths or
perspectives. This card can indicate a sense of uncertainty or doubt
about the future, as well as a need to clarify one's priorities and values
in relationships. It may also suggest a need to let go of rigid
expectations and to embrace spontaneity and flexibility in order to
adapt to changing circumstances. This card can also suggest a need
to communicate openly and honestly with one's partner in order to
build trust and strengthen the relationship.

Need to re-evaluate plans and goals, and consider alternative
paths or perspectives.
Sense of uncertainty or doubt about the future, and need to
clarify priorities and values in relationships.
Need to let go of rigid expectations and embrace spontaneity
and flexibility to adapt to changing circumstances.
Need for open and honest communication with one's partner to
build trust and strengthen the relationship.

Three of Wands

The Three of Wands in the upright position often indicates a period of
expansion and growth in a partnership, with a focus on exploration and
adventure. This card suggests a sense of optimism and excitement
about the future, as well as a willingness to explore new possibilities
and take calculated risks with a partner. It may indicate a desire for
independence and freedom within the relationship, as well as a need
for clear boundaries and communication. This card can also suggest a
need to balance one's own interests with those of the partnership in
order to maintain harmony and mutual respect.

Period of expansion and growth in a partnership, with a focus
on exploration and adventure.
Sense of optimism and excitement about the future, and
willingness to explore new possibilities and take calculated
risks with a partner.
Desire for independence and freedom within the relationship,
and need for clear boundaries and communication.
Need to balance one's own interests with those of the
partnership to maintain harmony and mutual respect.

The Three of Wands in the reversed position suggests a need to
re-evaluate the balance of power and the distribution of resources
within the relationship. This card can indicate a sense of imbalance or
inequality, as well as a need to establish clearer boundaries and
communication in order to build trust and respect. It may also suggest
a need to re-examine one's own motivations and desires within the

relationship, and to consider whether they align with the needs of the partnership. This card can also suggest a need to avoid impulsive or reckless behavior that may harm the relationship.

Need to re-evaluate the balance of power and distribution of resources within the relationship.
Sense of imbalance or inequality, and need to establish clearer boundaries and communication to build trust and respect.
Need to re-examine one's own motivations and desires within the relationship, and consider whether they align with the needs of the partnership.
Need to avoid impulsive or reckless behavior that may harm the relationship.

Four of Wands

The Four of Wands in the upright position often indicates a time of celebration, harmony, and stability in a partnership. This card suggests a strong foundation and a sense of security in the relationship, as well as a shared vision and commitment to each other's happiness and well-being. It may indicate a significant milestone or achievement in the relationship, such as a wedding, engagement, or the purchase of a home. This card can also suggest a need to celebrate and honor the positive aspects of the relationship, and to express gratitude and appreciation for one another.

Time of celebration, harmony, and stability in a partnership.
Strong foundation and sense of security in the relationship, with shared vision and commitment to each other's happiness and well-being.
Significant milestone or achievement in the relationship, such as a wedding, engagement, or purchase of a home.
Need to celebrate and honor the positive aspects of the relationship, and express gratitude and appreciation for one another.

The Four of Wands in the reversed position suggests a need to reassess the foundations of the relationship and address any underlying issues or conflicts. This card can indicate a lack of harmony or stability, as well as a need to establish clearer boundaries and expectations. It may also suggest a need to release any negative patterns or cycles in the relationship, and to work towards creating a more positive and supportive environment. This card can also suggest a need to avoid taking the relationship for granted, and to put in the effort to maintain the connection and spark.

> Need to reassess the foundations of the relationship and address any underlying issues or conflicts.
> Lack of harmony or stability, and need to establish clearer boundaries and expectations.
> Need to release negative patterns or cycles in the relationship, and work towards creating a more positive and supportive environment.
> Need to avoid taking the relationship for granted, and put in the effort to maintain the connection and spark.

Five of Wands

In matters of love and relationships, the Five of Wands in the upright position often indicates a period of conflict, competition, and tension. This card suggests that there may be disagreements or power struggles within the relationship, as well as a need to address and resolve any underlying issues. It may also indicate a need to set boundaries and communicate more clearly with your partner. This card can also suggest a need to approach the situation with a sense of playfulness and openness, and to avoid taking things too seriously.

> Period of conflict, competition, and tension within the relationship.
> Need to address and resolve underlying issues, and set clear boundaries.
> Need to communicate more clearly with your partner.
> Approach the situation with a sense of playfulness and

openness, and avoid taking things too seriously.

The Five of Wands in the reversed position suggests a resolution to conflicts and an easing of tensions. This card can indicate that you and your partner have found a way to work together and overcome any obstacles in the relationship. It may also suggest a need to forgive and let go of any past hurts or resentments, and to approach the relationship with a sense of cooperation and teamwork. This card can also suggest a need to maintain open and honest communication with your partner, and to avoid getting caught up in petty arguments or power struggles.

> Resolution to conflicts and easing of tensions in the relationship.
> Finding a way to work together and overcome obstacles.
> Need to forgive and let go of past hurts or resentments.
> Approach the relationship with a sense of cooperation and teamwork.
> Maintain open and honest communication, and avoid petty arguments or power struggles.

Six of Wands

The Six of Wands in the upright position often indicates a sense of victory, celebration, and success within the relationship. This card suggests that you and your partner have overcome challenges and are now experiencing a period of harmony, balance, and mutual respect. It may also indicate that you are feeling confident and proud of your relationship, and are eager to share your happiness with others. This card can also suggest a need to maintain a sense of balance and equality within the relationship, and to avoid becoming complacent or taking each other for granted.

> Sense of victory, celebration, and success within the relationship.
> Overcoming challenges and experiencing harmony, balance, and mutual respect.

Feeling confident and proud of the relationship, and eager to share your happiness with others.
Maintaining a sense of balance and equality, and avoiding complacency or taking each other for granted.

The Six of Wands in the reversed position suggests a need to be cautious and avoid getting too carried away with success. This card can indicate that you or your partner may be feeling overly confident or arrogant, and may need to take a step back and reassess the relationship. It may also suggest that there may be some underlying issues or imbalances that need to be addressed, and that you may need to work together to find a solution. This card can also suggest a need to avoid becoming too focused on external validation or the opinions of others, and to prioritize your own needs and values within the relationship.

Need to be cautious and avoid becoming too carried away with success.
Feeling overly confident or arrogant, and needing to reassess the relationship.
Addressing underlying issues or imbalances, and finding a solution together.
Avoiding becoming too focused on external validation or the opinions of others, and prioritizing your own needs and values within the relationship.

Seven of Wands

The Seven of Wands in the upright position suggests a need to stand up for oneself and assert boundaries. This card indicates a situation where one's relationship is being challenged by external forces, and it calls for a strong sense of self-confidence and courage to overcome them. The Seven of Wands may also suggest a need to assert oneself in a situation where one's partner is being dismissive or disrespectful.

Defending one's boundaries and standing up for oneself in a relationship.

Overcoming external obstacles or challenges with
self-confidence and courage.
Asserting oneself in a situation where one's partner is being
dismissive or disrespectful.
Facing opposition or competition for one's partner's affection.

The Seven of Wands in the reversed position suggests a need to step
back and reevaluate one's position in the relationship. This card may
indicate a situation where one is being defensive or overly aggressive,
and it may call for a more diplomatic or compromising approach. The
reversed Seven of Wands may also suggest a need to confront one's
own insecurities or doubts in order to regain confidence and improve
the relationship.

Stepping back and reevaluating one's position in the
relationship.
Taking a more diplomatic or compromising approach to resolve
conflicts.
Confronting one's own insecurities or doubts that may be
affecting the relationship.
Being defensive or overly aggressive towards one's partner.

<u>Eight of Wands</u>

The Eight of Wands in the upright position often indicates a period of
swift and decisive action. This card suggests that things are moving
quickly in your romantic life and that you may need to act fast to keep
up. It may indicate a sudden burst of passion or attraction, or a new
relationship that quickly becomes intense. This card can also suggest
a need for clear communication and honesty in relationships, as well
as a willingness to take risks and pursue new opportunities.

Swift and decisive action in matters of love and relationships.
Sudden burst of passion or attraction.
New relationship that quickly becomes intense.
Need for clear communication and honesty in relationships.
Willingness to take risks and pursue new opportunities.

The Eight of Wands in the reversed position suggests a need to slow down and take a more measured approach. This card can indicate a period of stagnation or lack of progress in your romantic life, or a feeling of being overwhelmed by the pace of things. It may also suggest a need for better communication and honesty in relationships, as well as a tendency to avoid confrontation or difficult conversations. This card can also suggest a need for patience and mindfulness, as well as a willingness to let go of control and trust in the flow of things.

> Need to slow down and take a more measured approach in matters of love and relationships.
> Period of stagnation or lack of progress in romantic life.
> Feeling overwhelmed by the pace of things.
> Need for better communication and honesty in relationships.
> Tendency to avoid confrontation or difficult conversations.
> Need for patience and mindfulness.
> Willingness to let go of control and trust in the flow of things.

<u>Nine of Wands</u>

The Nine of Wands in the upright position often indicates a need for perseverance and determination in the face of challenges. This card suggests that you may be feeling battle-worn and exhausted from past relationship struggles, but you have not given up. You are still standing and ready to fight for what you want. This card can also suggest that you are fiercely protective of your heart and your loved ones, and may have walls up to protect yourself from further hurt. It may indicate a need for boundaries in your relationships and a willingness to stand up for yourself.

> Perseverance and determination in the face of challenges.
> Feeling battle-worn and exhausted from past relationship struggles.
> Fiercely protective of your heart and loved ones.
> Walls up to protect yourself from further hurt.
> Need for boundaries in relationships.

Willingness to stand up for yourself.

The Nine of Wands in the reversed position suggests a need to let go of defensiveness and open yourself up to vulnerability. This card can indicate that you are feeling burned out and may be tempted to give up on finding love altogether. It may suggest a need to heal from past relationship wounds and let go of your guard. This card can also suggest a need to trust in your own resilience and ability to handle any challenges that may come your way.

Letting go of defensiveness and opening yourself up to vulnerability.
Feeling burned out and tempted to give up on finding love.
Healing from past relationship wounds.
Letting go of your guard.
Trusting in your own resilience and ability to handle challenges.

Ten of Wands

In matters of love and relationships, the Ten of Wands in the upright position can suggest a period of hard work and responsibility in a relationship. This card may indicate that one partner is taking on more than their fair share of the burden, leading to feelings of exhaustion or burnout. It may also suggest that the relationship has become weighed down by past issues or responsibilities, and there is a need to lighten the load or delegate tasks more evenly. Alternatively, the Ten of Wands can also suggest that the hard work and effort put into a relationship will ultimately pay off, leading to a sense of accomplishment and success.

Period of hard work and responsibility in a relationship.
Feeling weighed down by past issues or responsibilities.
One partner taking on more than their fair share of the burden.
Need to lighten the load or delegate tasks more evenly.
Hard work and effort will pay off, leading to a sense of accomplishment and success.

The Ten of Wands in the reversed position suggests a need to release burdens and let go of responsibilities in order to find more balance and freedom in a relationship. This card may indicate a need to examine where the relationship is feeling stifled or stagnant, and to identify ways to create more space for growth and exploration. It may also suggest that the hard work and effort put into the relationship has become unsustainable, and there is a need to let go of old patterns or expectations in order to move forward.

Release burdens and let go of responsibilities.
Examine where the relationship is feeling stifled or stagnant.
Create more space for growth and exploration.
Let go of old patterns or expectations in order to move forward.
Hard work and effort put into the relationship has become unsustainable.

Page of Wands

The Page of Wands in the upright position can suggest a period of excitement, passion, and creativity in a relationship. This card may indicate that new ideas or opportunities are emerging, and there is a sense of adventure and spontaneity in the relationship. It may also suggest that one or both partners are feeling confident and inspired, ready to take on new challenges and explore new horizons together. Alternatively, the Page of Wands can also suggest a need to balance this fiery energy with patience and groundedness, in order to avoid impulsive actions or conflicts.

Excitement, passion, and creativity in a relationship.
New ideas or opportunities emerging.
Sense of adventure and spontaneity.
Feeling confident and inspired, ready to take on new challenges.
Need to balance fiery energy with patience and groundedness.

The Page of Wands in the reversed position suggests a need to reignite passion and creativity in a relationship that has become stagnant or routine. This card may indicate a lack of excitement or enthusiasm, and a need to reconnect with the sense of adventure and spontaneity that brought the couple together in the first place. It may also suggest a need to let go of fears or doubts that may be holding the relationship back, and to embrace new opportunities or ways of being together.

Need to reignite passion and creativity in a stagnant relationship.
Lack of excitement or enthusiasm.
Reconnect with the sense of adventure and spontaneity.
Let go of fears or doubts that may be holding the relationship back.
Embrace new opportunities or ways of being together.

Knight of Wands

The Knight of Wands in the upright position suggests a passionate and adventurous energy in a relationship. This card may indicate a new relationship or phase of a current relationship that is marked by spontaneity, excitement, and a willingness to take risks. It may also suggest that one partner is taking on a more active, assertive role in the relationship, which can be invigorating or overwhelming depending on the situation. Alternatively, the Knight of Wands can also indicate a need to be mindful of impulsive behavior, and to channel the fiery energy of the relationship in a constructive way.

Passionate and adventurous energy in a relationship.
New relationship or phase of a relationship marked by spontaneity, excitement, and a willingness to take risks.
One partner taking on a more active, assertive role in the relationship.
Need to be mindful of impulsive behavior.
Channel fiery energy of the relationship in a constructive way.

The Knight of Wands in the reversed position suggests a need for patience and caution. This card may indicate that the energy of the relationship is moving too quickly, or that there is a need to slow down and take time to assess the situation. It may also suggest that one partner is behaving recklessly or selfishly, leading to conflict or mistrust. Alternatively, the reversed Knight of Wands can indicate a need to tap into one's own passion and assertiveness, and to take a more active role in the relationship in order to move it forward.

> Need for patience and caution.
> Energy of the relationship moving too quickly.
> One partner behaving recklessly or selfishly, leading to conflict or mistrust.
> Tap into one's own passion and assertiveness.
> Take a more active role in the relationship to move it forward.

<u>Queen of Wands</u>

The Queen of Wands in the upright position suggests a powerful and confident energy in relationships. This card may indicate that the querent or their partner embodies the qualities of the Queen of Wands - passionate, charismatic, and confident. This energy can bring excitement and enthusiasm to the relationship, and may indicate a time of creative or sexual exploration. However, the Queen of Wands can also indicate a need to balance this fiery energy with patience and compassion, as the intensity of this energy can sometimes lead to impulsive or reckless behavior.

> Powerful and confident energy in relationships.
> Passionate, charismatic, and confident partner or querent.
> Excitement and enthusiasm in the relationship.
> Time of creative or sexual exploration.
> Need to balance fiery energy with patience and compassion.

The Queen of Wands in the reversed position suggests a need to examine where one's confidence may be masking deeper insecurities or vulnerabilities. This card may indicate that the querent or their partner is struggling with issues of self-esteem or self-worth, and may be overcompensating with bravado or arrogance. The reversed Queen of Wands can also indicate a need to take a step back and reassess the relationship, as the intensity of the energy may be causing instability or emotional turbulence.

Examining where confidence may be masking deeper insecurities or vulnerabilities.
Struggling with issues of self-esteem or self-worth.
Overcompensating with bravado or arrogance.
Need to take a step back and reassess the relationship.
Intensity of energy may be causing instability or emotional turbulence.

King of Wands

The King of Wands in the upright position can suggest a confident and passionate partner who knows what they want and is not afraid to go after it. This card may indicate a relationship with someone who is a natural leader, highly independent, and often fiery and impulsive in their approach to love. It may also suggest a need for balance in the relationship, as the King of Wands can sometimes be overly focused on their own desires and goals. However, with clear communication and a willingness to compromise, this can be a successful and exciting relationship.

Confident and passionate partner.
Natural leader, highly independent, and fiery.
Need for balance in the relationship.
Successful and exciting relationship with clear communication and willingness to compromise.

The King of Wands in the reversed position can suggest a partner who is overly controlling or dominating, and may be prone to anger or volatility. This card may indicate a need for caution in the relationship, as the reversed King of Wands can sometimes represent a manipulative or abusive partner. Alternatively, it may suggest that the individual is struggling with their own sense of confidence and direction, leading to a lack of stability in their relationships.

Partner who is overly controlling or dominating, and prone to anger or volatility.
Need for caution in the relationship.
Manipulative or abusive partner.
Individual struggling with their own sense of confidence and direction, leading to a lack of stability in their relationships.

Meanings of the Minor Arcana: Swords

The suit of Swords is closely associated with the power of the mind, intellectual clarity, and rationality. It is often seen as a symbol of conflict, challenge, and difficulty, making it an important symbol for understanding the complexities of romantic interpersonal relationships.

At its core, the suit of Swords relates to the ways in which we communicate and interact with one another in the context of relationships. It can represent the clarity and understanding that can arise through honest and direct communication, as well as the painful misunderstandings and conflicts that can arise when communication breaks down.

One of the key ways in which the Swords relate to love and romance is through their association with intellectual clarity and honesty. Just as the sword can cut through confusion and uncertainty, so too can honest communication help to clarify feelings, desires, and intentions within romantic relationships. By fostering open and direct communication, couples can build a stronger foundation of trust and understanding, even in the face of challenging circumstances.

However, the Swords can also represent the potential for conflict and disagreement within romantic relationships. When communication breaks down or misunderstandings arise, it can be easy for emotions to escalate and tempers to flare. In these instances, the Swords can be a symbol of the sharp words and hurtful actions that can damage even the strongest of relationships.

Swords can also be a symbol of the painful emotional experiences that can arise in the context of breakups, divorce, and other forms of romantic separation. Swords can cut through physical barriers, and so, they can also represent the painful emotional wounds that can arise when a relationship comes to an end.

Overall, the suit of Swords is a complex and multifaceted symbol that speaks to the challenges and opportunities inherent in romantic interpersonal relationships. Whether it is through honest communication, painful conflict and separation, or the ongoing effort required to maintain a healthy relationship, the Swords serve as a reminder of the power of our words and actions to shape the course of our lives and our relationships with others.

Let us now dive into the divinatory meanings of the Swords as they relate to love and relationships!

<u>Ace of Swords</u>

In matters of love and relationships, the Ace of Swords in the upright position can suggest a new beginning or fresh start in communication or mental clarity within a relationship. This card may indicate a need for clear and honest communication, and a willingness to address any conflicts or challenges that may arise. It may also suggest a need for intellectual stimulation or a shared interest in a mental pursuit to keep the relationship fresh and engaging. Alternatively, the Ace of Swords can also indicate a time of mental breakthroughs or epiphanies that lead to a greater understanding or awareness of the relationship.

> A new beginning or fresh start in communication or mental clarity within a relationship.
> A need for clear and honest communication.
> Addressing conflicts or challenges with intellectual precision.
> Intellectual stimulation or shared interests in a mental pursuit.
> Time of mental breakthroughs or epiphanies that lead to a greater understanding of the relationship.

The Ace of Swords in the reversed position suggests a need for caution and careful consideration before making any important decisions or engaging in difficult conversations. This card may indicate a tendency towards aggression or impulsiveness, leading to conflicts or misunderstandings. It may also suggest a need to clarify any misunderstandings or miscommunications before they escalate further.

Need for caution and careful consideration before making important decisions or engaging in difficult conversations.
Tendency towards aggression or impulsiveness, leading to conflicts or misunderstandings.
Need to clarify any misunderstandings or miscommunications before they escalate further.

Two of Swords

The Two of Swords in the upright position can suggest a need to make a difficult decision or choice regarding a relationship. This card may indicate a situation where the individual is feeling stuck or uncertain about their path forward in the relationship. It may also suggest a need to balance intellect and emotions in order to make the best decision. Alternatively, the Two of Swords can also indicate a period of temporary stalemate or truce in a relationship, where both parties are choosing to avoid confrontation or conflict rather than address underlying issues.

Need to make a difficult decision or choice regarding a relationship.
Feeling stuck or uncertain about the path forward in the relationship.
Balancing intellect and emotions to make the best decision.
Temporary stalemate or truce in the relationship.

The Two of Swords in the reversed position suggests a need to confront and address underlying issues in a relationship in order to move forward. This card may indicate a situation where the individual has been avoiding conflict or difficult conversations, leading to an unhealthy pattern of communication. It may also suggest a need to let go of indecisiveness and commit to a clear path forward in the relationship.

Need to confront and address underlying issues in a relationship.

Avoiding conflict or difficult conversations may lead to
unhealthy patterns of communication.
Let go of indecisiveness and commit to a clear path forward in
the relationship.

Three of Swords

The Three of Swords in the upright position often indicates heartbreak,
betrayal, and emotional pain. This card suggests the experience of a
painful breakup, loss, or separation. It may also suggest a sense of
isolation and loneliness, as well as a need to grieve and process
emotional wounds. This card can also indicate the need for honest
communication and confrontation in order to heal and move forward.

Heartbreak, betrayal, and emotional pain.
Painful breakup, loss, or separation.
Sense of isolation and loneliness.
Need to grieve and process emotional wounds.
Honest communication and confrontation to heal and move
forward.

The Three of Swords in the reversed position suggests the possibility
of healing and recovery from emotional pain. This card can indicate
the need to release past wounds and resentments, and to let go of
negative emotions and patterns that prevent growth and healing. It
may also suggest the possibility of reconciliation or forgiveness, as
well as the potential for new relationships and experiences.

Healing and recovery from emotional pain.
Releasing past wounds and resentments.
Letting go of negative emotions and patterns.
Possibility of reconciliation or forgiveness.
Potential for new relationships and experiences.

Four of Swords

The Four of Swords in the upright position often indicates the need for a temporary break or hiatus from romantic pursuits. This card suggests a time to step back from dating or pursuing a relationship, and instead focus on self-care and personal growth. It may also indicate the need to heal from past emotional wounds, and to cultivate a sense of inner peace and balance before entering into a new romantic partnership. This card can also suggest the potential for spiritual growth and enlightenment through self-reflection and self-love.

> Need for a temporary break or hiatus from romantic pursuits.
> Stepping back from dating or pursuing a relationship to focus on self-care and personal growth.
> Healing from past emotional wounds before entering into a new partnership.
> Cultivating a sense of inner peace and balance before pursuing a new relationship.
> Potential for spiritual growth and enlightenment through self-reflection and self-love.

The Four of Swords in the reversed position suggests the possibility of restlessness and impatience in romantic pursuits. This card can indicate a tendency to rush into relationships without proper self-care and introspection, and a reluctance to take the time to cultivate a strong sense of self before pursuing a romantic partnership. It may also suggest the need to address unresolved emotional issues or conflicts from past relationships in order to move forward in a healthy way. This card can also suggest the potential for inner turmoil and unrest in relationships without proper self-care and healing.

> Restlessness and impatience in romantic pursuits.
> Tendency to rush into relationships without proper self-care and introspection.
> Reluctance to take the time to cultivate a strong sense of self before pursuing a romantic partnership.

Need to address unresolved emotional issues or conflicts from past relationships.
Potential for inner turmoil and unrest in relationships without proper self-care and healing.

Five of Swords

In matters of love and relationships, the Five of Swords in the upright position often indicates conflict and disharmony in a romantic partnership. This card suggests the potential for power struggles, manipulation, and betrayal within the relationship. It may indicate the need for clear communication and setting healthy boundaries in order to resolve conflicts and build a stronger partnership. This card can also suggest the possibility of letting go of a relationship that is no longer serving you in a positive way, in order to move on to healthier, more fulfilling connections.

Conflict and disharmony in a romantic partnership.
Potential for power struggles, manipulation, and betrayal within the relationship.
Need for clear communication and setting healthy boundaries to resolve conflicts and build a stronger partnership.
Possibility of letting go of a relationship that is no longer serving you in a positive way.
Moving on to healthier, more fulfilling connections.

The Five of Swords in the reversed position suggests the potential for healing and resolution in a previously conflicted relationship. This card can indicate a willingness to let go of power struggles and manipulation, and to instead approach the partnership with compassion, empathy, and forgiveness. It may also suggest the need to acknowledge and address any past hurts or negative patterns within the relationship in order to move towards a more positive and harmonious connection. This card can also suggest the potential for learning valuable lessons through difficult experiences within the relationship.

Potential for healing and resolution in a previously conflicted relationship.
Willingness to let go of power struggles and manipulation, and approach the partnership with compassion, empathy, and forgiveness.
Acknowledgment and addressing of past hurts or negative patterns within the relationship.
Moving towards a more positive and harmonious connection.
Learning valuable lessons through difficult experiences within the relationship.

Six of Swords

The Six of Swords in the upright position often indicates a period of transition and moving on from past challenges or difficulties. This card suggests the possibility of leaving behind a turbulent or stagnant relationship and embarking on a journey towards a more positive and harmonious connection. It may indicate the need to let go of past hurts and resentments in order to move forward with a clear and open heart. This card can also suggest the potential for finding a partner who is supportive, understanding, and compassionate, and who helps to guide you towards a brighter future.

Transition and moving on from past challenges or difficulties.
Leaving behind a turbulent or stagnant relationship and embarking on a journey towards a more positive and harmonious connection.
Letting go of past hurts and resentments in order to move forward with a clear and open heart.
Potential for finding a partner who is supportive, understanding, and compassionate, and who helps to guide you towards a brighter future.

The Six of Swords in the reversed position suggests the potential for difficulty in moving on from past relationships or patterns of behavior that are no longer serving you. This card can indicate the need for introspection and self-reflection in order to identify and address any underlying emotional wounds or negative beliefs that may be preventing you from finding happiness and fulfillment in your relationships. It may also suggest the need for patience and perseverance in order to navigate through challenging times within a current partnership, with the hope of ultimately reaching a more positive and harmonious connection.

Difficulty in moving on from past relationships or patterns of behavior that are no longer serving you.
Need for introspection and self-reflection in order to identify and address underlying emotional wounds or negative beliefs.
Patience and perseverance in order to navigate through challenging times within a current partnership.
Hope of ultimately reaching a more positive and harmonious connection.

Seven of Swords

The Seven of Swords in the upright position often indicates the potential for deceit, betrayal, or dishonesty within a partnership. This card suggests the need to be cautious and aware of any red flags or signs of manipulation or dishonesty from a current or potential partner. It may indicate the importance of being honest and transparent in your own actions and intentions, and avoiding any temptations to engage in deceitful behavior. This card can also suggest the need for setting healthy boundaries and taking steps to protect yourself from any potential harm or hurt within a relationship.

Potential for deceit, betrayal, or dishonesty within a partnership.
Need to be cautious and aware of any red flags or signs of manipulation or dishonesty from a current or potential partner.
Importance of being honest and transparent in your own actions and intentions.
Need for setting healthy boundaries and taking steps to protect yourself from any potential harm or hurt within a relationship.

The Seven of Swords in the reversed position suggests the potential for a resolution or coming to terms with a past betrayal or deceit within a partnership. This card can indicate the need for forgiveness and letting go of any lingering resentment or bitterness towards a former partner or situation. It may also suggest the importance of being honest and transparent in your own actions and intentions within a current or future relationship, and avoiding any temptation to engage in dishonest or manipulative behavior.

> Resolution or coming to terms with a past betrayal or deceit within a partnership.
> Need for forgiveness and letting go of any lingering resentment or bitterness towards a former partner or situation.
> Importance of being honest and transparent in your own actions and intentions within a current or future relationship.
> Avoiding any temptation to engage in dishonest or manipulative behavior.

Eight of Swords

The Eight of Swords in the upright position often indicates feelings of being trapped, restricted, or powerless within a partnership. This card suggests the need to examine any limiting beliefs or patterns that may be contributing to feelings of insecurity or self-doubt in relationships. It may indicate the importance of communication and expressing your needs and desires within a partnership, as well as taking active steps to assert your independence and autonomy. This card can also suggest the need for self-reflection and personal growth in order to break free from any negative or self-defeating patterns in relationships.

> Feelings of being trapped, restricted, or powerless within a partnership.
> Need to examine any limiting beliefs or patterns that may be contributing to feelings of insecurity or self-doubt in relationships.
> Importance of communication and expressing your needs and desires within a partnership.

Taking active steps to assert your independence and autonomy.
Need for self-reflection and personal growth in order to break free from any negative or self-defeating patterns in relationships.

The Eight of Swords in the reversed position suggests a potential for breaking free from negative or self-defeating patterns within a partnership. This card can indicate the importance of taking action and asserting your independence and autonomy within a relationship, as well as communicating your needs and desires. It may also suggest a newfound sense of confidence and empowerment in relationships, as well as a willingness to take risks and explore new experiences.

Breaking free from negative or self-defeating patterns within a partnership.
Taking action and asserting your independence and autonomy within a relationship.
Communicating your needs and desires.
Newfound sense of confidence and empowerment in relationships.
Willingness to take risks and explore new experiences.

Nine of Swords

The Nine of Swords in the upright position often indicates feelings of anxiety, worry, or fear within a partnership. This card suggests the need to examine any underlying issues or conflicts that may be contributing to these negative emotions, as well as the importance of seeking support and guidance from trusted friends or professionals. It may indicate a need to let go of any unrealistic expectations or fears of rejection within relationships, as well as the importance of cultivating self-compassion and self-care. This card can also suggest a need for honest and open communication within a partnership in order to address any concerns or conflicts.

Feelings of anxiety, worry, or fear within a partnership.

Examination of underlying issues or conflicts that may be contributing to negative emotions.
Importance of seeking support and guidance from trusted friends or professionals.
Letting go of unrealistic expectations or fears of rejection within relationships.
Cultivating self-compassion and self-care.
Need for honest and open communication within a partnership to address concerns or conflicts.

The Nine of Swords in the reversed position suggests a potential for overcoming negative emotions and fears within a partnership. This card can indicate the importance of taking action to address any underlying issues or conflicts, as well as the importance of cultivating self-compassion and self-care. It may also suggest a newfound sense of clarity and perspective within a partnership, as well as the potential for growth and transformation.

Overcoming negative emotions and fears within a partnership.
Taking action to address underlying issues or conflicts.
Cultivating self-compassion and self-care.
Newfound sense of clarity and perspective within a partnership.
Potential for growth and transformation.

<u>Ten of Swords</u>

In matters of love and relationships, the Ten of Swords in the upright position often indicates a painful ending or betrayal within a partnership. This card suggests the need to acknowledge and accept the reality of the situation, as well as the importance of allowing oneself to grieve and heal. It may indicate a need to let go of any blame or resentment towards oneself or others, and to seek support and guidance from trusted friends or professionals during this difficult time. This card can also suggest the potential for transformation and rebirth, as well as the importance of learning from past experiences in order to move forward.

Painful ending or betrayal within a partnership.
Acknowledgment and acceptance of the reality of the situation.
Allowing oneself to grieve and heal.
Letting go of blame or resentment towards oneself or others.
Seeking support and guidance from trusted friends or professionals.
Potential for transformation and rebirth through learning from past experiences.

The Ten of Swords in the reversed position suggests the potential for healing and recovery after a painful ending or betrayal within a partnership. This card can indicate the importance of taking time to process and reflect on the experience, as well as the potential for newfound strength and resilience. It may also suggest the need to let go of any lingering negative emotions or attachments, and to focus on self-care and personal growth.

Healing and recovery after a painful ending or betrayal within a partnership.
Taking time to process and reflect on the experience.
Newfound strength and resilience.
Letting go of lingering negative emotions or attachments.
Focus on self-care and personal growth.

Page of Swords

The Page of Swords in the upright position often indicates a sharp, intellectual approach to love. This card suggests a desire for communication and honesty in relationships, as well as a need for mental stimulation and challenges. It may indicate a curiosity and fascination with new ideas and perspectives, and a willingness to explore uncharted territory. This card can also suggest a need to be independent and assertive in relationships, as well as a desire for a partner who values intelligence and wit.

Sharp, intellectual approach to love.
Desire for communication and honesty in relationships.

Need for mental stimulation and challenges.
Curiosity and fascination with new ideas and perspectives.
Willingness to explore uncharted territory.
Need to be independent and assertive in relationships.
Desire for a partner who values intelligence and wit.

The Page of Swords in the reversed position suggests a need to be cautious and thoughtful in communication. This card can indicate a tendency to be argumentative or defensive in relationships, as well as a fear of vulnerability or emotional intimacy. It may also suggest a need to examine and challenge one's own beliefs and perspectives in order to find true understanding and connection with a partner. This card can also suggest a desire to find a sense of inner clarity and focus in relationships.

Need to be cautious and thoughtful in communication.
Tendency to be argumentative or defensive in relationships.
Fear of vulnerability or emotional intimacy.
Need to examine and challenge one's own beliefs and perspectives.
Desire to find a sense of inner clarity and focus in relationships.

Knight of Swords

The Knight of Swords in the upright position often indicates a fast-paced, action-oriented approach to love. This card suggests a desire for intellectual stimulation and challenge in relationships, as well as a need for clear communication and honesty. It may indicate a partner or potential partner who is intelligent, ambitious, and focused on their goals. This card can also suggest a need for independence and freedom in relationships, as well as a desire for excitement and adventure.

Fast-paced, action-oriented approach to love.
Desire for intellectual stimulation and challenge in relationships.
Need for clear communication and honesty.

Partner or potential partner who is intelligent, ambitious, and focused.
Need for independence and freedom in relationships.
Desire for excitement and adventure.

The Knight of Swords in the reversed position suggests a need to slow down and approach love and relationships with more thoughtfulness and patience. This card can indicate a tendency to rush into relationships or decisions without considering the consequences or emotions involved. It may also suggest a need for clearer communication and more openness in relationships, as well as a desire for more stability and security.

Need to slow down and approach love and relationships with more thoughtfulness and patience.
Tendency to rush into relationships or decisions without consideration.
Need for clearer communication and more openness in relationships.
Desire for more stability and security.
Potential for conflicts or misunderstandings due to lack of clarity or honesty.
Need for better planning and foresight in relationships.

Queen of Swords

The Queen of Swords in the upright position often indicates a need for clarity and honesty in communication. This card suggests a highly intellectual and analytical approach to love, and a preference for clear, concise, and direct communication. It may indicate a need for independence and self-sufficiency in relationships, as well as a desire for a partner who is intellectually stimulating and can engage in deep conversations. This card can also suggest a need for emotional detachment and objectivity in order to make clear decisions and avoid being swept away by emotions.

Clarity and honesty in communication.

Intellectual and analytical approach to love.
Desire for independence and self-sufficiency in relationships.
Need for a partner who is intellectually stimulating.
Emotional detachment and objectivity.

The Queen of Swords in the reversed position suggests a need for more compassion, empathy, and emotional connection. This card can indicate a tendency to be too harsh or critical in communication, and a need to soften one's approach and be more understanding of others. It may also suggest a need to let go of rigid thinking and be more open to new perspectives and ideas. This card can also suggest a need to balance intellectual and emotional aspects of oneself in order to form deeper and more fulfilling relationships.

Need for more compassion, empathy, and emotional connection.
Softening one's approach and being more understanding of others.
Letting go of rigid thinking and being more open to new perspectives and ideas.
Balancing intellectual and emotional aspects of oneself.
Forming deeper and more fulfilling relationships.

King of Swords

The King of Swords in the upright position often represents a highly rational and analytical approach to love. This card suggests the importance of clear communication, logical thinking, and a pragmatic approach to problem-solving in relationships. It may indicate the need to balance emotions with reason and to make decisions based on logic rather than purely on feelings. This card can also suggest the importance of intelligence, knowledge, and intellectual compatibility in relationships.

Highly rational and analytical approach to love.
Importance of clear communication and logical thinking.
Pragmatic approach to problem-solving in relationships.

Balancing emotions with reason.
Importance of intelligence, knowledge, and intellectual
compatibility.

The King of Swords in the reversed position suggests a tendency to be overly critical or judgmental in relationships. This card can indicate a lack of emotional connection or empathy, and a need to balance intellect with compassion. It may also suggest a need to be more open and vulnerable in relationships, and to communicate feelings rather than solely relying on reason. This card can also suggest the importance of kindness, sensitivity, and emotional intelligence in relationships.

Being overly critical or judgmental in relationships.
Lack of emotional connection or empathy.
Balancing intellect with compassion.
Need to be more open and vulnerable in relationships.
Importance of kindness, sensitivity, and emotional intelligence.

Meanings of the Minor Arcana: Cups

The suit of Cups is often associated with emotions, intuition, and relationships. More than any other suit in the tarot deck, the Cups exemplify the concept of love and human relationships. The Cups represent the element of water, which is a symbol of the unconscious mind, creativity, and the emotional landscape of our lives.

The Cups are often associated with love and all of the emotional aspects of relationships, including the less than positive aspects. The card of the Ace of Cups, for example, is seen as a symbol of new beginnings, emotional fulfillment, and spiritual connection. This card can indicate the start of a new relationship or a deepening of an existing one. The Four of Cups, on the other hand, can indicate a time of emotional withdrawal, apathy, or disconnection. This card can suggest a need for introspection and self-care in order to strengthen emotional bonds with others.

The Cups can also provide guidance on breakups, divorce, and other forms of relationship dissolution. The Five of Cups, for example, is often interpreted as a symbol of grief, loss, and disappointment. This card can indicate a period of emotional pain and mourning following a breakup or divorce. The Ten of Cups, on the other hand, can represent a sense of emotional completion, harmony, and fulfillment. This card can indicate a period of healing and growth following a difficult breakup or divorce.

As we will soon see, the suit of Cups can provide valuable insights into the many facets of romantic interpersonal relationships. From new beginnings and emotional fulfillment to breakup and divorce, the Cups offer guidance on the emotional landscape of our lives and relationships. Whether seeking to deepen a current relationship or navigate a difficult breakup, the Cups can provide valuable guidance and support.

Let us now dive into the divinatory meanings of the Cups as they relate to love and relationships!

<u>Ace of Cups</u>

In matters of love and relationships, the Ace of Cups in the upright position indicates the beginning of a new emotional journey or a renewal of feelings in an existing relationship. This card suggests the presence of pure, unconditional love and emotional fulfillment. It can represent a new romantic relationship or a deepening of an existing one, and a strong spiritual connection between partners. It is important to be open and receptive to the love and positive emotions that are available to you at this time.

> The beginning of a new emotional journey or renewal of feelings in an existing relationship.
> Pure, unconditional love and emotional fulfillment.
> A new romantic relationship or deepening of an existing one.
> A strong spiritual connection between partners.
> Being open and receptive to the love and positive emotions that are available to you.

The Ace of Cups in the reversed position suggests blocked emotions, lack of emotional fulfillment, and a difficulty in expressing feelings or receiving love. This card can indicate a need to heal past emotional wounds and to let go of any negative emotions or beliefs that are hindering your ability to connect with others. It is important to work towards emotional balance and to be honest with yourself and your partner about your true feelings.

> Blocked emotions, lack of emotional fulfillment.
> Difficulty in expressing feelings or receiving love.
> A need to heal past emotional wounds and let go of negative emotions or beliefs.
> Working towards emotional balance.
> Being honest with yourself and your partner about your true feelings.

<u>Two of Cups</u>

The Two of Cups represents the beginning of a deep emotional connection and the potential for a loving partnership. This card suggests a mutual attraction and a sense of balance and harmony between two people. It can indicate the start of a new romance, a strengthening of an existing relationship, or the possibility of a deep and meaningful connection with someone special. This card encourages open communication, trust, and mutual respect in order to create a strong and loving relationship.

> The beginning of a deep emotional connection and potential for a loving partnership.
> A mutual attraction and sense of balance and harmony between two people.
> The start of a new romance, or a strengthening of an existing relationship.
> The possibility of a deep and meaningful connection with someone special.
> Open communication, trust, and mutual respect are essential for a strong and loving relationship.

The Two of Cups reversed may suggest a lack of connection or emotional imbalance between partners. It can indicate a lack of trust or communication, or a difficulty in finding common ground. This card may also suggest the need to let go of a past relationship or to reassess the current one in order to move forward. It is important to be honest with oneself and one's partner in order to create a healthy and loving relationship.

> A lack of connection or emotional imbalance between partners.
> A lack of trust or communication, or difficulty in finding common ground.
> The need to let go of a past relationship or reassess the current one in order to move forward.

Honesty with oneself and one's partner is necessary for a healthy and loving relationship.
This card may also suggest the potential for conflicts or challenges in a current relationship that need to be addressed in order to move forward.

<u>Three of Cups</u>

The Three of Cups card in the upright position suggests a time of celebration, joy, and connection with loved ones. This card can indicate a deepening of existing relationships or the potential for new romantic connections. It is a time to let loose, have fun, and enjoy the company of those you care about. This card can also indicate a need to balance your social life with your romantic relationships and to create harmony between the two.

> A time of celebration, joy, and connection with loved ones.
> Deepening of existing relationships or potential for new romantic connections.
> Letting loose, having fun, and enjoying the company of those you care about.
> Balancing your social life with your romantic relationships and creating harmony between the two.

The Three of Cups card in the reversed position suggests a time of conflict, jealousy, or gossip within your social or romantic circles. This card can indicate a need to distance yourself from toxic friendships or relationships and to focus on those who truly care about you. It may also indicate a need to reassess your priorities and create more balance in your life, as you may be neglecting your romantic relationships or other important areas of your life.

> Conflict, jealousy, or gossip within your social or romantic circles.
> A need to distance yourself from toxic friendships or relationships and focus on those who truly care about you.
> Reassessing your priorities and creating more balance in your

life.
Neglecting your romantic relationships or other important areas
of your life.

<u>Four of Cups</u>

The Four of Cups in the upright position suggests a period of apathy,
boredom, or disillusionment. You may feel as though you have
everything you need in your relationship, but there is still something
missing. It is important to take a step back and evaluate your feelings
in order to understand what it is that you truly desire in your love life.
This card can indicate a need to explore new opportunities or
perspectives in your relationships in order to reignite the spark and
passion. This card can also indicate a need to be cautious of
becoming too complacent or taking your partner for granted. It may be
time to open up to new experiences and take some risks in order to
bring more excitement and joy to your relationship.

A period of apathy, boredom, or disillusionment in your
relationship.
Feeling as though something is missing.
Taking a step back and evaluating your feelings in order to
understand what you truly desire in your love life.
Exploring new opportunities or perspectives in your
relationships to reignite the spark and passion.

The Four of Cups in the reversed position suggests a newfound
appreciation for the love and connection that you have in your life. You
may have gone through a period of feeling uninspired or unfulfilled in
your relationships, but you are now ready to embrace the love and
happiness that is available to you. This card can also indicate a need
to express gratitude and appreciation to your partner, and to be open
to new opportunities and experiences that will bring you closer
together. This card can also indicate a need to let go of any negative
or limiting beliefs that are holding you back in your relationships, and
to embrace a more positive and optimistic outlook. It is time to let go of

the past and move forward with a renewed sense of hope and enthusiasm for your love life.

A newfound appreciation for the love and connection in your life.
Embracing the love and happiness that is available to you.
Expressing gratitude and appreciation to your partner.
Being open to new opportunities and experiences that will bring you closer together.

Five of Cups

In matters of love and relationships, the Five of Cups in the upright position can indicate a time of sadness, grief, or disappointment. It can suggest that you are dwelling on past failures or losses in your relationships, rather than focusing on the present or future. You may have experienced a recent breakup, a loss of a loved one, or a betrayal, and you are still mourning and grieving the past.

This card can also indicate the need for forgiveness, both for yourself and for others, in order to move on from a difficult or painful experience. It is important to find healthy ways to process your emotions and to seek support from loved ones. You may feel like your heart has been shattered into a million pieces, and you can't seem to move on from the pain and hurt.

However, the Five of Cups also reminds you that even though you are in a period of sadness and loss, there is still hope for the future. The two upright cups on the card represent the possibility of new love and relationships, and the hooded figure in the background suggests that help and support are available if you are willing to seek it out.

Sadness, grief, or disappointment in love or relationships.
Dwelling on past failures or losses.
The need for forgiveness to move on from a difficult or painful experience.
Finding healthy ways to process emotions and seeking support

from loved ones.

The Five of Cups in the reversed position suggests a time of healing, forgiveness, and moving forward. It can indicate a willingness to let go of past hurts and to focus on the positive aspects of your relationships. This card can also suggest the potential for new love or emotional connections, as you open yourself up to new possibilities. It is important to stay grounded in reality and to avoid getting swept away by idealized fantasies or unrealistic expectations.

Healing, forgiveness, and moving forward in love or relationships.
Letting go of past hurts and focusing on the positive.
Potential for new love or emotional connections.
Staying grounded in reality and avoiding idealized fantasies or unrealistic expectations.

Six of Cups

The Six of Cups in the upright position often indicates a nostalgic or sentimental outlook on love. This card suggests a return to past relationships or memories, and a longing for the innocence and purity of childhood. It may indicate a strong connection to someone from your past, or a desire to find a partner who embodies the qualities of a childhood crush or friend. This card can also suggest a need for emotional healing and forgiveness in relationships, as well as a desire for a stable and nurturing home life. It can also indicate a desire to revisit the past or reconnect with an old flame

Nostalgia or sentimentality towards love and relationships.
A return to past relationships or memories.
Longing for the innocence and purity of childhood.
Strong connection to someone from your past.
Desire for emotional healing and forgiveness in relationships.
Need for a stable and nurturing home life.
A desire to revisit the past or reconnect with an old flame.

The Six of Cups in the reversed position suggests a need to let go of the past and move forward with a new outlook on love. This card can indicate a tendency to dwell on past relationships or memories, and a reluctance to embrace new experiences or partners. It may also suggest a need for emotional healing and forgiveness in order to release negative patterns or cycles in relationships. This card can also suggest a desire to find a sense of inner childlike joy and playfulness in relationships.

Letting go of the past and embracing new experiences.
Releasing negative patterns or cycles in relationships.
Finding emotional healing and forgiveness.
Reluctance to embrace new experiences or partners.
Desire for a sense of inner childlike joy and playfulness in relationships.

<u>Seven of Cups</u>

The Seven of Cups in the upright position suggests a need for clarity and focus. This card can indicate a time of confusion or indecision, where you may be facing multiple options or choices in your romantic life. It is important to take the time to evaluate your options carefully and to prioritize what truly matters to you in a relationship. This card can also indicate a need to be cautious of illusions or unrealistic expectations in love and to remain grounded in reality. This card can also indicate a need to explore your desires and fantasies, but to be aware of the consequences and to make sure that your actions align with your values.

A need for clarity and focus in romantic matters.
Facing multiple options or choices in love.
Taking the time to evaluate options carefully and prioritizing what truly matters.
Being cautious of illusions or unrealistic expectations in love.
Remaining grounded in reality.

The Seven of Cups in the reversed position suggests a time of clarity and decision-making. This card can indicate a release from confusion or uncertainty in your romantic life and a newfound sense of clarity about what you truly want in a relationship. It is important to take action towards your goals and to be confident in your choices. This card can also indicate a need to let go of unrealistic expectations or fantasies in love and to focus on building realistic and meaningful connections. This card can also indicate a need to be aware of your emotions and to process any feelings of disappointment or disillusionment in past relationships before moving forward.

      A time of clarity and decision-making in romantic matters.
      A release from confusion or uncertainty in love.
      A newfound sense of clarity about what you truly want in a relationship.
      Taking action towards your goals and being confident in your choices.
      Letting go of unrealistic expectations or fantasies in love and focusing on building realistic and meaningful connections.

Eight of Cups

The Eight of Cups in the upright position suggests a need to leave behind a situation or relationship that no longer serves you. This card can indicate a feeling of dissatisfaction or boredom in your current partnership, and a desire for something more fulfilling. It may be time to take a risk and pursue a new love interest, or to focus on your own personal growth and development. While leaving behind the familiar may be scary, it can ultimately lead to greater happiness and satisfaction in the long run.

      Leaving behind a situation or relationship that no longer serves you.
      Feeling dissatisfied or bored in your current partnership.
      Desiring something more fulfilling.
      Taking a risk and pursuing a new love interest.
      Focusing on personal growth and development.

This card can also indicate the need to be honest with yourself and your partner about your feelings, and to communicate openly in order to create a healthy and balanced relationship.

The Eight of Cups in the reversed position suggests a hesitation or resistance to let go of a situation or relationship that is no longer serving you. This card can indicate a fear of the unknown or a reluctance to take risks in matters of the heart. It may be important to take a step back and evaluate your current situation in order to determine what changes need to be made to create a more fulfilling relationship. While change can be scary, it is often necessary in order to grow and find greater happiness.

Hesitation or resistance to let go of a situation or relationship that is no longer serving you.
Fear of the unknown or reluctance to take risks in matters of the heart.
Needing to take a step back and evaluate your current situation.
Making changes in order to create a more fulfilling relationship.
Embracing change in order to find greater happiness.
This card can also indicate the need to work on developing a stronger sense of self-worth and self-love before pursuing new relationships.

Nine of Cups

The Nine of Cups in the upright position often indicates a sense of emotional fulfillment and satisfaction. This card suggests that your desires and wishes in love and relationships have been met or are soon to be met. It may indicate a period of joy and contentment in your current relationship, or the arrival of a new partner who embodies your ideal mate. This card can also suggest a need for balance and harmony in relationships, as well as a desire for a fulfilling and meaningful emotional connection.

Emotional fulfillment and satisfaction in love and relationships.

Desires and wishes being met or soon to be met.
Joy and contentment in a current relationship or the arrival of a new partner.
Need for balance and harmony in relationships.
Desire for a fulfilling and meaningful emotional connection.

The Nine of Cups in the reversed position suggests a sense of disappointment or unfulfillment in love and relationships. This card can indicate a lack of emotional satisfaction, or the feeling that your desires and wishes in love and relationships are not being met. It may also suggest a need for self-reflection and introspection, in order to identify and address any underlying issues or negative patterns that may be contributing to this sense of unfulfillment. This card can also suggest a need for open communication and honest expression of emotions in relationships.

Sense of disappointment or unfulfillment in love and relationships.
Lack of emotional satisfaction or desires and wishes not being met.
Need for self-reflection and introspection to address underlying issues or negative patterns.
Need for open communication and honest expression of emotions in relationships.

Ten of Cups

In matters of love and relationships, the Ten of Cups in the upright position often indicates a deep sense of emotional fulfillment and happiness in all areas of life. This card suggests a harmonious and loving family life, a sense of belonging, and a strong emotional connection with loved ones. It may indicate a period of peace and contentment in your current relationship, or the arrival of a new partner who embodies your ideal vision of a family life. This card can also suggest a need for emotional healing and forgiveness in relationships, as well as a desire for a stable and nurturing home life.

Deep sense of emotional fulfillment and happiness in love and relationships.
Harmonious and loving family life, sense of belonging and strong emotional connection.
Peace and contentment in a current relationship or the arrival of a new partner.
Need for emotional healing and forgiveness in relationships.
Desire for a stable and nurturing home life.

The Ten of Cups in the reversed position suggests a disruption of emotional harmony and fulfillment. This card can indicate a breakdown in family relationships or a lack of emotional connection with loved ones. It may also suggest a need for self-reflection and introspection, in order to identify and address any underlying issues or negative patterns that may be contributing to this disruption. This card can also suggest a need for open communication and honest expression of emotions in relationships.

Disruption of emotional harmony and fulfillment in love and relationships.
Breakdown in family relationships or lack of emotional connection with loved ones.
Need for self-reflection and introspection to address underlying issues or negative patterns.
Need for open communication and honest expression of emotions in relationships.

Page of Cups

The Page of Cups in the upright position often indicates a new emotional connection or opportunity for love. This card suggests a sense of innocence, purity, and openness to love, as well as a willingness to explore and express one's emotions. It may indicate the arrival of a new romantic interest or a renewed sense of passion in an existing relationship. This card can also suggest a need for creativity and imagination in relationships, as well as a desire for a deeper understanding of one's own emotional needs and desires.

New emotional connection or opportunity for love.
Innocence, purity, and openness to love.
Willingness to explore and express one's emotions.
Arrival of a new romantic interest or a renewed sense of
passion.
Need for creativity and imagination in relationships.
Desire for a deeper understanding of one's own emotional
needs and desires.

The Page of Cups in the reversed position suggests a need to focus on emotional maturity and growth. This card can indicate a tendency towards emotional immaturity or manipulation in relationships, as well as a lack of understanding or communication regarding one's own emotions. It may also suggest a need for self-reflection and introspection, in order to identify and address any underlying emotional blocks or negative patterns that may be contributing to these issues. This card can also suggest a need to be cautious and discerning when it comes to new romantic opportunities.

Need to focus on emotional maturity and growth.
Tendency towards emotional immaturity or manipulation in
relationships.
Lack of understanding or communication regarding one's own
emotions.
Need for self-reflection and introspection to address underlying
emotional blocks or negative patterns.
Need to be cautious and discerning when it comes to new
romantic opportunities.

Knight of Cups

The Knight of Cups in the upright position often indicates a romantic and passionate individual who is willing to take risks in the pursuit of love. This card suggests a sense of adventure, creativity, and charm in relationships, as well as a desire to express and explore one's emotions fully. It may indicate the arrival of a new romantic interest who is passionate and confident, or a renewal of passion in an existing relationship. This card can also suggest a need for balance between emotion and action, as well as a desire for a deep, spiritual connection with a partner.

> Romantic and passionate individual willing to take risks in the pursuit of love.
> Sense of adventure, creativity, and charm in relationships.
> Desire to express and explore one's emotions fully.
> Arrival of a new romantic interest who is passionate and confident, or a renewal of passion in an existing relationship.
> Need for balance between emotion and action.
> Desire for a deep, spiritual connection with a partner.

The Knight of Cups in the reversed position suggests a need to be cautious and avoid impulsiveness in matters of the heart. This card can indicate a tendency towards manipulation or deception in relationships, as well as a lack of commitment or follow-through. It may also suggest a need for self-reflection and introspection, in order to identify and address any underlying emotional blocks or negative patterns that may be contributing to these issues. This card can also suggest a need to focus on personal growth and emotional maturity before pursuing new romantic opportunities.

> Need to be cautious and avoid impulsiveness in matters of the heart.
> Tendency towards manipulation or deception in relationships.
> Lack of commitment or follow-through.
> Need for self-reflection and introspection to address underlying emotional blocks or negative patterns.
> Need to focus on personal growth and emotional maturity before pursuing new romantic opportunities.

Queen of Cups

The Queen of Cups in the upright position often indicates a nurturing and intuitive individual who is deeply in touch with their emotions. This card suggests a strong sense of empathy and compassion in relationships, as well as a desire to create a loving and supportive environment for loved ones. It may indicate a need to prioritize emotional well-being and self-care in relationships, as well as a desire for deep emotional connections with partners. This card can also suggest a need for introspection and reflection, in order to better understand one's own emotional needs and boundaries.

Nurturing and intuitive individual deeply in touch with their emotions.
Strong sense of empathy and compassion in relationships.
Desire to create a loving and supportive environment for loved ones.
Need to prioritize emotional well-being and self-care in relationships.
Desire for deep emotional connections with partners.
Need for introspection and reflection to understand emotional needs and boundaries.

The Queen of Cups in the reversed position suggests a need to balance emotional needs and boundaries in relationships. This card can indicate a tendency towards emotional codependency or neglect of one's own needs in order to please others. It may also suggest a need for clear communication and boundaries in relationships, in order to avoid misunderstandings and emotional conflicts. This card can also suggest a need for self-care and emotional healing, in order to avoid being overwhelmed or drained by emotional demands.

Need to balance emotional needs and boundaries in relationships.
Tendency towards emotional codependency or neglect of one's own needs in order to please others.
Need for clear communication and boundaries in relationships to avoid misunderstandings and emotional conflicts.
Need for self-care and emotional healing to avoid being overwhelmed or drained by emotional demands.

<u>King of Cups</u>

The King of Cups in the upright position often indicates a mature and emotionally stable individual who is comfortable expressing their feelings and nurturing their relationships. This card suggests a strong sense of empathy and compassion, as well as a desire to create a harmonious and loving environment for loved ones. It may indicate a need to balance emotional needs and boundaries in relationships, in order to avoid being overwhelmed or drained by emotional demands. This card can also suggest a need for clear communication and honest expression of feelings, in order to build trust and intimacy in relationships.

> Mature and emotionally stable individual comfortable expressing feelings and nurturing relationships.
> Strong sense of empathy and compassion.
> Desire to create a harmonious and loving environment for loved ones.
> Need to balance emotional needs and boundaries in relationships.
> Clear communication and honest expression of feelings to build trust and intimacy in relationships.

The King of Cups in the reversed position suggests a need for emotional healing and self-reflection in order to address emotional imbalances and conflicts. This card can indicate a tendency towards emotional repression or overindulgence, as well as a difficulty in expressing feelings or establishing emotional boundaries in relationships. It may also suggest a need for greater self-awareness and introspection, in order to understand one's own emotional needs and limitations in relationships.

> Need for emotional healing and self-reflection to address emotional imbalances and conflicts.
> Tendency towards emotional repression or overindulgence.
> Difficulty expressing feelings or establishing emotional boundaries in relationships.

Need for greater self-awareness and introspection to understand emotional needs and limitations in relationships.

Meanings of the Minor Arcana: Pentacles

The suit of Pentacles is closely associated with material wealth, stability, and abundance. As such, it can be viewed as a symbol of the practical aspects of romantic relationships, including finances, stability, and security.

One of the primary ways in which the pentacle relates to love and romance is through its association with financial stability and security. For many couples, financial stability is a key component of a healthy and fulfilling relationship, allowing them to plan for the future and build a life together. The Pentacles can also represent the tangible aspects of love, such as gifts, vacations, and other material expressions of affection.

However, the pentacle can also represent the potential for conflict and disagreement over financial matters within romantic relationships. When couples disagree over how to manage their finances or how to prioritize their spending, it can lead to tension and discord within the relationship.

Pentacles can also be a symbol of the practical considerations that arise in the context of breakups, divorce, and other forms of romantic separation. Issues such as dividing assets and debts, negotiating alimony or child support, and other financial matters can be some of the most challenging and emotionally charged aspects of any breakup or divorce.

In the context of marriage, the pentacle can represent the importance of building a stable and secure foundation for the relationship. By prioritizing financial stability and planning for the future, couples can build a stronger sense of trust and confidence in their relationship, even in the face of challenges and difficulties.

The pentacle can also be a symbol of the importance of putting in the work to build a healthy and fulfilling relationship. Just as building wealth requires discipline, hard work, and strategic planning, so too does building a successful romantic relationship require effort and dedication.

Whether it is through building a stable foundation for a healthy relationship, navigating the practical considerations of a breakup or divorce, or working together to achieve shared financial goals, the pentacle serves as a reminder of the tangible and material aspects of our romantic interpersonal relationships.

Let us now dive into the divinatory meanings of the Pentacles as they relate to love and relationships!

<u>Ace of Pentacles</u>

In matters of love and relationships, the Ace of Pentacles in the upright position often indicates the beginning of a new and prosperous relationship, one that has the potential to bring material and emotional abundance. This card suggests the possibility of a stable and secure relationship built on trust, mutual respect, and shared values. It may indicate the start of a new phase in a current relationship or a new relationship that will provide a strong foundation for growth and long-term commitment. This card can also suggest a need to prioritize practical considerations such as financial stability and security in relationships.

> Beginning of a new and prosperous relationship.
> Stable and secure relationship built on trust and shared values.
> Potential for material and emotional abundance.
> Need to prioritize practical considerations in relationships.
> New phase in a current relationship or a new relationship that provides a strong foundation for growth and long-term commitment.

The Ace of Pentacles in the reversed position suggests a need to reevaluate practical considerations and priorities in relationships. This card can indicate a lack of stability and security in relationships, or a lack of focus on the practical aspects of a relationship. It may also suggest a need to let go of materialistic or superficial values that may be hindering the growth and development of a relationship. This card can also suggest the need to focus on building emotional and spiritual abundance in relationships.

Reevaluation of practical considerations and priorities in relationships.
Lack of stability and security in relationships or lack of focus on practical aspects.
Letting go of materialistic or superficial values hindering growth and development.
Need to focus on building emotional and spiritual abundance in relationships.
Potential for missed opportunities for growth and abundance in relationships.

Two of Pentacles

The Two of Pentacles in the upright position suggests a need for balance and flexibility. This card indicates that there may be multiple demands or priorities in your love life that require juggling, and that you must be adaptable in order to keep everything in harmony. This card can also suggest the need for open communication and the ability to adjust to changes in your relationship in order to maintain stability. It may indicate the importance of finding a partner who shares similar values and priorities.

Balance and flexibility in love and relationships.
Juggling multiple demands or priorities.
Adaptability in order to keep everything in harmony.
Open communication and ability to adjust to changes in your relationship.
Importance of finding a partner who shares similar values and priorities.

The Two of Pentacles in the reversed position suggests a lack of balance and stability. This card can indicate that you may be struggling to manage multiple demands or priorities, leading to a sense of chaos or overwhelm in your love life. It may suggest a need to prioritize and simplify your commitments, or to delegate tasks in order to free up more time for your relationship. This card can also indicate the importance of setting clear boundaries and learning to say no in order to maintain your own well-being.

Lack of balance and stability in love and relationships.
Struggling to manage multiple demands or priorities.
Need to prioritize and simplify commitments.
Importance of setting clear boundaries and learning to say no.
Delegation of tasks in order to free up more time for your relationship.

Three of Pentacles

The Three of Pentacles in the upright position suggests a need for collaboration and cooperation. This card indicates that working together as a team can lead to success and stability in relationships. It can also suggest the need for open and clear communication, as well as the importance of setting goals and working towards them together. The Three of Pentacles can also indicate the need to seek out and learn from experienced and knowledgeable individuals in order to improve and strengthen relationships.

Collaboration and cooperation in relationships.
Working together as a team for success and stability.
Open and clear communication.
Setting goals and working towards them together.
Seeking out and learning from experienced and knowledgeable individuals.

The Three of Pentacles in the reversed position suggests a lack of collaboration and cooperation. This card can indicate a breakdown in communication or a lack of willingness to work together towards common goals. It may also suggest a need for individual growth and development in order to improve relationships. The reversed Three of Pentacles can also indicate a need to be wary of those who may not have your best interests at heart.

Lack of collaboration and cooperation in relationships.
Breakdown in communication or lack of willingness to work together.
Need for individual growth and development.
Wary of those who may not have your best interests at heart.

Four of Pentacles

The Four of Pentacles in the upright position often indicates a need for stability and security in partnerships. This card suggests a desire to hold onto what you have and protect your heart, possibly due to past hurts or fears of being hurt. It may indicate a reluctance to share your feelings or vulnerability with your partner, or a need for control in the relationship. This card can also suggest a focus on material possessions and financial security as a way to create a stable foundation for a partnership.

A need for stability and security in partnerships.
Desire to hold onto what you have and protect your heart.
Reluctance to share your feelings or vulnerability with your partner.
Need for control in the relationship.
Focus on material possessions and financial security.

The Four of Pentacles in the reversed position suggests a need to let go of the need for control and to be more open and vulnerable in partnerships. This card can indicate a fear of change or taking risks in relationships, and a tendency to hold onto past hurts or negative patterns. It may also suggest a need to let go of the focus on material possessions and financial security as the foundation of a partnership, and instead focus on emotional and spiritual connection.

Letting go of the need for control and being more open and vulnerable in partnerships.
Fear of change or taking risks in relationships.
Holding onto past hurts or negative patterns.
Letting go of the focus on material possessions and financial security as the foundation of a partnership.
Focusing on emotional and spiritual connection.

Five of Pentacles

In matters of love and relationships, the Five of Pentacles in the upright position suggests feelings of isolation or exclusion. This card can indicate a sense of being left out in the cold or feeling like an outsider in a relationship or social setting. It may also suggest financial or material difficulties affecting the relationship, creating feelings of insecurity or inadequacy. However, this card can also indicate the potential for growth and strength through adversity, as it encourages you to seek out support and rely on inner resources to overcome challenges.

Feelings of isolation or exclusion in a relationship or social setting.
Financial or material difficulties affecting the relationship.
Insecurity or inadequacy in the relationship.
Potential for growth and strength through adversity.
Encouragement to seek out support and rely on inner resources.

The Five of Pentacles in the reversed position suggests overcoming feelings of isolation or exclusion. This card can indicate a newfound sense of belonging or acceptance in a relationship or social setting. It may also suggest a resolution to financial or material difficulties that were previously affecting the relationship. However, this card can also indicate the need to avoid becoming too attached to material possessions or external validation in the relationship.

Overcoming feelings of isolation or exclusion in a relationship

or social setting.
Newfound sense of belonging or acceptance in the relationship.
Resolution to financial or material difficulties affecting the relationship.
Avoiding attachment to material possessions or external validation in the relationship.

Six of Pentacles

The Six of Pentacles in the upright position suggests a giving and receiving of love and support in a relationship. This card may indicate a balanced and harmonious partnership, where both partners are contributing equally to the relationship. It may also suggest generosity and kindness towards your partner, as well as a willingness to share your resources and time. This card can also indicate a need for financial stability and security in relationships, and a desire for a comfortable and secure home life.

Giving and receiving of love and support in a relationship.
Balanced and harmonious partnership.
Generosity and kindness towards your partner.
Willingness to share your resources and time.
Need for financial stability and security in relationships.
Desire for a comfortable and secure home life.

The Six of Pentacles in the reversed position suggests a lack of balance and fairness in the relationship. This card may indicate one partner giving more than they receive, or vice versa, leading to feelings of resentment or inequality. It may also suggest a need to reassess the dynamics of the relationship and establish clear boundaries and expectations. This card can also indicate a need to let go of financial or material concerns and focus on building emotional wealth and intimacy in the relationship.

Lack of balance and fairness in the relationship.
One partner giving more than they receive, or vice versa.

Feelings of resentment or inequality.
Need to reassess the dynamics of the relationship.
Establishment of clear boundaries and expectations.
Focus on building emotional wealth and intimacy in the
relationship.

<u>Seven of Pentacles</u>

The Seven of Pentacles in the upright position suggests a need to take
a step back and assess the current state of the relationship. This card
indicates a period of waiting and patience, as well as a desire for
growth and development. It may suggest a need to reevaluate the
effort and resources being put into the relationship, and to consider
whether they are yielding the desired results. This card can also
indicate a need for a more balanced give-and-take in the relationship,
as well as a focus on building a solid foundation for the future.

Assessing the current state of the relationship.
Waiting and patience.
Desire for growth and development.
Reevaluating effort and resources being put into the
relationship.
Need for a balanced give-and-take in the relationship.
Focus on building a solid foundation for the future.

The Seven of Pentacles in the reversed position suggests a need to
take action and make changes in the relationship. This card indicates
a period of impatience and frustration, as well as a lack of progress or
growth. It may suggest a need to let go of outdated beliefs or habits
that are hindering the relationship, and to embrace new perspectives
and approaches. This card can also indicate a need for greater
communication and collaboration in the relationship, as well as a focus
on creating a more fulfilling and satisfying dynamic.

Taking action and making changes in the relationship.
Impatience and frustration.
Lack of progress or growth.

Letting go of outdated beliefs or habits.
Embracing new perspectives and approaches.
Greater communication and collaboration in the relationship.

<u>Eight of Pentacles</u>

The Eight of Pentacles in the upright position often indicates a focus on commitment, dedication, and hard work in building a strong and fulfilling relationship. This card suggests that you are willing to put in the time and effort necessary to create a solid foundation for your partnership. It may also indicate a need for patience and perseverance in matters of love, and a willingness to learn and grow alongside your partner.

Focus on commitment, dedication, and hard work in building a relationship.
Willingness to put in the time and effort necessary for a strong partnership.
Need for patience and perseverance in matters of love.
Willingness to learn and grow alongside your partner.

The Eight of Pentacles in the reversed position suggests a need to re-evaluate your approach to love and commitment. This card can indicate a tendency to be too focused on work or other outside interests, and neglecting your relationship. It may also suggest a need to examine your priorities and values in order to create a better balance between your personal and romantic life.

Need to re-evaluate your approach to love and commitment.
Tendency to be too focused on work or other outside interests.
Neglecting your relationship.
Need to examine your priorities and values to create a better balance between your personal and romantic life.

<u>Nine of Pentacles</u>

The Nine of Pentacles in the upright position suggests a strong focus on independence and self-sufficiency. This card suggests that you are content with your current relationship status and enjoy being single, or that you are in a committed relationship where you and your partner have a healthy balance of independence and togetherness. It may indicate that you have worked hard to achieve financial stability, and that this is a priority in your love life as well. This card can also suggest that you are attracting partners who value your independence and appreciate your self-reliance.

Strong focus on independence and self-sufficiency.
Contentment with being single or in a healthy, balanced relationship.
Prioritizing financial stability in your love life.
Attracting partners who value your independence and self-reliance.

The Nine of Pentacles in the reversed position suggests a need to reassess your priorities and goals in love. This card can indicate that you are overly focused on material possessions and financial stability, to the detriment of your relationships. It may also suggest that you are feeling lonely or isolated, and that you need to focus on building more connections and socializing. This card can also suggest a need to let go of perfectionism and control in your relationships, and to be more open to vulnerability and emotional intimacy.

Reassessing priorities and goals in love.
Being overly focused on material possessions and financial stability.
Feeling lonely or isolated, and needing to build connections.
Letting go of perfectionism and control in relationships.
Being more open to vulnerability and emotional intimacy.

Ten of Pentacles

In matters of love and relationships, the Ten of Pentacles in the upright position represents a strong commitment to building a lasting and secure relationship. This card indicates a sense of fulfillment and satisfaction in a stable and harmonious partnership. It suggests the presence of strong family values and a desire for a traditional and secure home life. The Ten of Pentacles also suggests financial security and stability, which can contribute to a sense of ease and contentment in relationships. This card can indicate a strong connection with family members and a desire for a partner who shares these values.

Strong commitment to building a lasting and secure relationship.
Fulfillment and satisfaction in a stable and harmonious partnership.
Presence of strong family values and a desire for a traditional and secure home life.
Financial security and stability contributing to ease and contentment in relationships.
Strong connection with family members and a desire for a partner who shares these values.

The Ten of Pentacles in the reversed position suggests instability and uncertainty in a relationship. This card can indicate a lack of commitment and a sense of restlessness or dissatisfaction in a partnership. It may also suggest financial instability and a lack of security, which can contribute to tension and conflict in relationships. The reversed Ten of Pentacles can also indicate a need to reassess one's values and priorities in order to build a more stable and fulfilling partnership.

Instability and uncertainty in a relationship.
Lack of commitment and a sense of restlessness or dissatisfaction in a partnership.
Financial instability and a lack of security contributing to tension and conflict in relationships.
Need to reassess one's values and priorities in order to build a more stable and fulfilling partnership.

<u>Page of Pentacles</u>

The Page of Pentacles in the upright position suggests a grounded and practical approach to love. This card may indicate the beginning of a new relationship or a time of exploration and learning within a current partnership. It can also suggest a focus on building a stable and secure home life with a partner, as well as a desire for material comfort and security. The Page of Pentacles in this context may also indicate a need to be patient and take things slow, as well as a focus on communication and honesty in relationships.

> Grounded and practical approach to love.
> Beginning of a new relationship or time of exploration and learning.
> Focus on building a stable and secure home life.
> Desire for material comfort and security.
> Need to be patient and take things slow.
> Focus on communication and honesty in relationships.

The Page of Pentacles in the reversed position suggests a need to reassess one's priorities and values in love. This card may indicate a lack of focus or direction in relationships, as well as a tendency to become overly materialistic or superficial. It can also suggest a need to work on developing self-worth and confidence before pursuing a new relationship, as well as a need to let go of past hurts and resentments. The Page of Pentacles in this context may also indicate a need to be more open-minded and adaptable in relationships.

> Need to reassess priorities and values in love.
> Lack of focus or direction in relationships.
> Tendency to become overly materialistic or superficial.
> Need to work on developing self-worth and confidence.
> Need to let go of past hurts and resentments.
> Need to be more open-minded and adaptable in relationships.

<u>Knight of Pentacles</u>

The Knight of Pentacles suggests a practical and responsible approach. This card indicates a reliable and steady partner who values security and stability in relationships. It may also suggest a need to focus on the material aspects of a relationship, such as financial stability and practical considerations. This card can indicate a willingness to work hard to build a solid foundation for a long-term commitment, and a commitment to making things work in the long run.

> A practical and responsible approach to love and relationships.
> Reliability and steadiness as a partner.
> A focus on the material aspects of a relationship.
> Willingness to work hard to build a solid foundation for a long-term commitment.
> Commitment to making things work in the long run.

The reversed Knight of Pentacles suggests a need to reevaluate priorities and expectations. This card can indicate a lack of spontaneity or a tendency to become too focused on the practical aspects of a relationship, at the expense of emotional connection and intimacy. It may also suggest a need to find balance between work and personal life, and a need to let go of rigid expectations and embrace change.

> Reevaluation of priorities and expectations.
> Lack of spontaneity or focus on practical aspects at the expense of emotional connection and intimacy.
> Finding balance between work and personal life.
> Letting go of rigid expectations and embracing change.

Queen of Pentacles

The Queen of Pentacles in the upright position often indicates a strong, nurturing, and practical approach to love. This card suggests a deep connection to the earth and the natural world, as well as a desire for stability and security in relationships. It may indicate a strong attachment to material comforts and a desire for financial stability as a foundation for a long-lasting partnership. This card can also suggest a need for practicality and groundedness in relationships, as well as a desire for loyalty and commitment.

Strong, nurturing, and practical approach to love.
Deep connection to the earth and the natural world.
Desire for stability and security in relationships.
Strong attachment to material comforts and financial stability.
Need for practicality and groundedness in relationships.
Desire for loyalty and commitment.

The Queen of Pentacles in the reversed position suggests a need to focus on emotional and spiritual connections over material comforts. This card can indicate a tendency to prioritize wealth and status over love and emotional fulfillment, as well as a lack of emotional depth in relationships. It may also suggest a need to address any fears or insecurities around financial stability, and to work on developing a more balanced approach to love and money. This card can also suggest a need for self-care and nurturing in order to attract and maintain a healthy and fulfilling partnership.

Need to focus on emotional and spiritual connections over material comforts.
Tendency to prioritize wealth and status over love and emotional fulfillment.
Lack of emotional depth in relationships.
Need to address fears or insecurities around financial stability.
Work on developing a more balanced approach to love and money.
Need for self-care and nurturing to attract and maintain a healthy partnership.

<u>King of Pentacles</u>

The King of Pentacles in the upright position suggests stability, security, and a commitment to building a strong foundation. This card represents a mature, responsible, and dependable partner who values the practical aspects of a relationship, such as financial security and stability. The King of Pentacles may indicate a focus on material comforts and luxury, and a desire for a comfortable and abundant lifestyle with their partner. This card can also suggest a need for balance between work and home life, as well as a need for quality time with their partner.

Stability, security, and commitment.
A mature, responsible, and dependable partner.
Valuing the practical aspects of a relationship, such as financial security and stability.
A focus on material comforts and luxury.
A desire for a comfortable and abundant lifestyle with their partner.
A need for balance between work and home life.
A need for quality time with their partner.

The King of Pentacles in the reversed position may indicate a lack of stability or a focus on material possessions over emotional connection. This card can suggest a partner who is overly concerned with work or financial success, and may neglect their relationship as a result. The reversed King of Pentacles can also indicate a lack of responsibility or dependability, and a tendency to avoid commitment. This card may also suggest a need to reassess priorities and focus on building a stronger emotional connection with their partner.

Lack of stability or a focus on material possessions over emotional connection.
A partner who is overly concerned with work or financial success, and may neglect their relationship as a result.
A lack of responsibility or dependability.
A tendency to avoid commitment.
A need to reassess priorities and focus on building a stronger emotional connection with their partner.

Love Spreads

Using Tarot card spreads specifically made for love readings is a popular way to seek insight into the questions one might have about their love life. These spreads can help provide clarity and guidance around questions very specifically related to love, romance, and relationships. In this section, we'll explore three tarot love spreads that can be used to answer common questions about love and relationships.

The first spread is the Past-Present-Future spread. This spread is helpful for gaining insight into how past experiences and decisions are impacting your current love life, and what the future may hold. To begin, shuffle the deck and lay three cards face down in a row, representing the past, present, and future. Turn the cards over one by one and interpret them in relation to the question being asked.

For example, if you're asking about a current relationship, the past card may represent past experiences that are impacting the relationship, the present card may represent the current state of the relationship, and the future card may represent what lies ahead for the relationship.

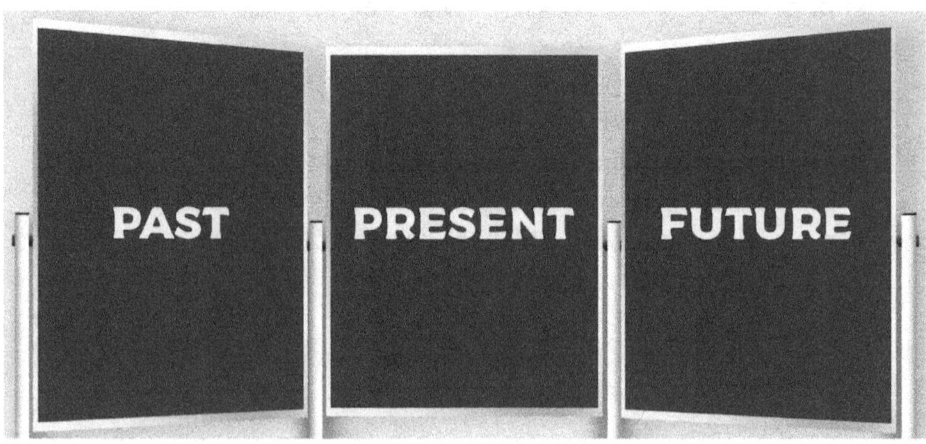

To gain even more clarity, you don't have to limit yourself to one card per section. For example, using two cards to represent the past, two to represent the present, and two to represent the future can give you a more robust image of what is going on in the relationship over time.

The second spread is the Relationship Potential Spread. This spread can be used to gain insight into the potential of a new relationship. To begin, shuffle the deck and lay out six cards in the shape of a pyramid. You will have 3 rows of cards: 3 cards in the bottom row, 2 cards in the middle row, and then 1 card at the top, forming the shape of a triangle or pyramid.

We start at the top, laying down the first card, which represents the overall energy or theme of the reading. This card will pertain to the energy of the relationship as a whole. The second row will have two cards: one representing you, the other, your partner. At the bottom row, we will lay down three cards. The first of the three cards laid down represents the current state of the relationship, the second of the three cards in that row represents the obstacles or challenges to the relationship, and the last card in that row represents the potential future of the relationship. Note: although the following picture shows an order to the laying down of the cards, you do not need to follow that exact order. As long as the meanings of the positions are taken into account, which card you lay down first or the order in which you place them down is not necessarily important.

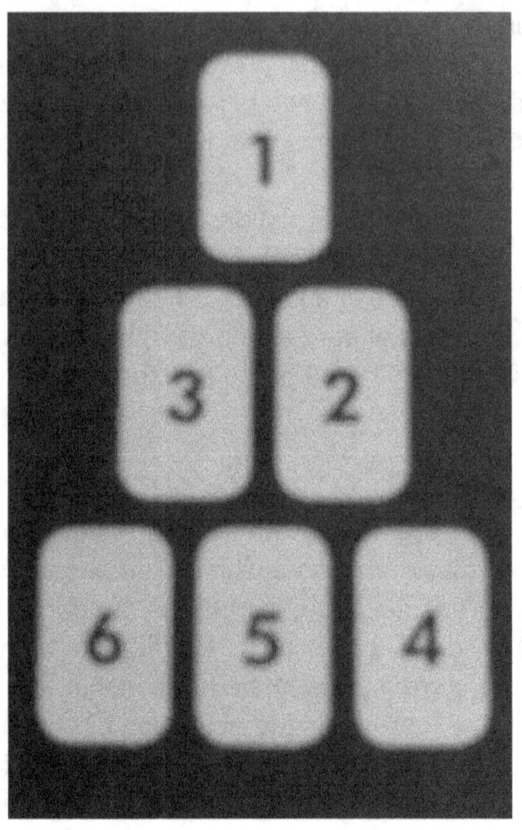

The third spread is the Love Triangle Spread. This spread can be used to gain insight into a situation where there may be competition or conflict between two potential partners. To begin, shuffle the deck and lay out three cards in a row, the first representing you, the second, your current partner, and the third card representing the third party. Interpret each card individually, and then consider how the three cards relate to one another. This spread can help shed light on the dynamics at play in a love triangle, and provide guidance on how to navigate the situation.

Again, with this spread, you are not limited to the order in which you place the cards down, nor the number of cards used. If you want to use 2 cards per position, or even more, you are free to do that. If you are a beginner though, I suggest you start with one card per position.

When using tarot spreads for love readings, it's important to keep in mind that the cards are simply a tool for gaining insight and guidance. While the cards may provide helpful information and guidance, ultimately, the decisions you make in your love life are up to you. Trust your intuition and use the cards as a tool for gaining deeper understanding and clarity around your romantic relationships.

Conclusion

As we have just seen, reading tarot cards for love and relationships is actually more straightforward than we once thought. Interpreting the love meanings of tarot cards is a powerful tool for gaining insight and guidance on matters related to the heart, as well as all other aspects of interpersonal connections.

One of the main benefits of using tarot for matters of the heart is that it allows us to see beyond our own biases and preconceived notions. By stepping outside of ourselves and examining our situations from a different perspective, we can gain new insights and ideas that we may not have considered before. This can be especially helpful in situations where emotions are running high and it may be difficult to see things clearly.

Another benefit of using tarot for matters of the heart is that it can provide us with a sense of clarity and direction. When we are struggling with a relationship issue, it can be easy to feel lost and unsure of what to do next. Tarot can offer us guidance and help us to see a path forward, even when things feel uncertain.

Of course, it's important to remember that tarot is just one tool in our arsenal when it comes to navigating relationships. It should never be used as a substitute for communication, therapy, or other forms of support. However, when used in conjunction with these other resources, tarot can be a powerful tool for gaining insight and clarity.

In the end, it's important to remember that relationships are complex and multifaceted, and there are no easy answers or quick fixes. However, by using tarot to tap into our intuition and gain new perspectives, we can become more empowered in our relationships and more confident in our ability to navigate the ups and downs of love and romance.

So if you're struggling with a relationship issue or simply looking for a way to gain deeper insight into your love life, don't hesitate to turn to the tarot for guidance. With practice and patience, the use of your own intuition, and with the help of this little book, I think you can continue to gain a deeper understanding of yourself and your chosen partner or partners!

About the Author

Celeste Randall is a tiny but mighty force to be reckoned with in the world of metaphysical and New Age literature. When she's not communing with the cosmos, you can find her at home surrounded by her two trusty feline companions - a pair of Oriental Shorthairs named Harut and Marut - and deep in thought about the mysteries of the universe.

As a self-proclaimed Tarot enthusiast, Law of Attraction believer, astrology aficionado, and numerology nerd, Celeste has made it her mission to share her knowledge and insights with the world. Her books are a treasure trove of wisdom for anyone seeking a deeper understanding of the universe and their place in it.

But don't be fooled by her ethereal musings and otherworldly pursuits – Celeste is a college-educated powerhouse who knows how to get things done. Majoring in Communications with an emphasis in Journalism, Celeste found her calling within the occult during a college house party where she had her first fortune read by a Tarot reader the host provided as entertainment. She was hooked and had to learn more from that day forward!

When she's not writing or consulting her crystal ball, she's running her own freelance e-commerce business from the comfort of her cozy home in Indiana, USA. She's a true modern-day mystic, with a laptop instead of a cauldron… although, on any given day, you will definitely also find her using a cauldron!

If you're one of the many curious individuals looking to unlock the secrets of the universe, Celeste's books are must-reads. She's got the experience, the wit, and the insight to guide you on your journey – and who knows, you might even discover a few new things about yourself along the way.

Here are some of the other titles in Celeste's arsenal of works that you might be interested in, dear reader!

Quick and Dirty Tarot
Quick and Dirty Manifestation
The Lover's Path: Reading Tarot for Love and Relationships
How Does He Feel About Me? Reading for the Most Popular Question in Tarot
Simple Symbols: Taking a Detailed Look at the Symbolism of Tarot
Forensic Tarot: Using the Tarot to Solve True Crime Mysteries

www.ingramcontent.com/pod-product-compliance
Lightning Source LLC
Chambersburg PA
CBHW071059250726
48662CB00019B/1506